WAY STATION
&
WHAT DOES A QUESTION WEIGH?

Way Station
&
What Does A Question Weigh?

Plays
by

WES PAYTON

A
BOOKS

Adelaide Books
New York / Lisbon
2019

WAY STATION
&
WHAT DOES A QUESTION WEIGH?

Plays

By Wes Payton

Published by Adelaide Books, New York / Lisbon
adelaidebooks.org

Editor-in-Chief
Stevan V. Nikolic

For any information, please address Adelaide Books
at info@adelaidebooks.org

or write to:

Adelaide Books
244 Fifth Ave. Suite D27
New York, NY, 10001

ISBN-10: 1-950437-49-3

ISBN-13: 978-1-950437-49-8

Printed in the United States of America

For Professor David Radavich—thank you for your encouragement during the writing of my first play.

For the members of Three Cat Productions—thank you for your enthusiasm during the workshopping and staged readings of these two plays.

Way Station

A Play
by

WES PAYTON

WAY STATION
(A writer walks into a bar.)

Characters

Frieze/Prisoner #655321—a has-been writer in his fifties (and thirties in scenes III) whose misanthropy has led to a hermitic life

Ease —a street person in his forties who's amiable despite his hardscrabble lifestyle

Sleaze —an alluring woman in her twenties (and forties in scenes I) who is new to the city and new to her job as Cheese's assistant

Cheese/Nutritionist —a seasoned publisher in his fifties who's as optimistic as he is absent-minded (a jailer in scenes II— could be played by a woman)

Louise —a beguiling woman in her thirties who is as attractive as she is clever

Wheeze —a somewhat successful writer in his fifties (and thirties in scenes III) whose long career belies his dearth of talent

Geeze —an avuncular and well-respected writer in his sixties whose drunkenness is the hallmark of Cheese's parties

Please/Steward —a surly bartender in his forties (a jailer in scenes II)

Stage

The action takes place in an unassuming corner tavern today and twenty years ago. The barroom remains unchanged in the odd numbered scenes, with the entrance stage left and the bar and exit to a backroom stage right. Tables and chairs occupy center stage. The cell in the second scene of each act is a single lit area in the middle of the barroom.

ACT ONE

Scene I
(Frieze stands, unsure of himself, at the entrance to the tavern.
Ease approaches.)

Frieze

(To Ease.) Hey, do you want to have a drink with me?

Ease

Ease What's that? Do I know you or something?

Frieze

No, and I'm not queer—just socially inexpert, as I'm sure
you've deduced by now. I don't have any friends around here,
and I used to frequent this tavern, but that was a long time
ago, and I'll be leaving soon, so I thought I'd stop by for one
last drink, although now that I'm here…anyway, I'll pay for
your drink.

Ease

Sure, I guess. What the hell, right? My throat's a little dry.

Frieze

(The two enter and sit down at a table.) Okay then, this table will do. What'll you have, a beer? You look like a beer drinker.

Ease

This is a classy place. I walk by here all the time, but I've never been inside—nice ambiance.

Frieze

It has a certain understated, rustic charm, though it could do with some updating. It looks exactly the same as it did twenty years ago.

Ease

I wonder what kind of food they serve here. I bet they got some good eats. The only food my regular bar has is pork rinds.

Frieze

What is a pork rind exactly?

Ease

Fried hog skin.

Frieze

Doesn't sound too healthy.

Ease

Nah, but neither is drinking booze.

Frieze

I'll grant you that—everything in moderation I suppose. Besides, what the fuck do I care if people choose to die fat nd middle-aged?

Ease

Uh, sure. Anyway, I think I'll order something, you know, highbrow…like a seven-and- seven.

Frieze

(Shouting to the bartender who is tallying receipts behind the bar.) Barkeep, two seven- and-sevens, posthaste. (To Ease.) It seems I just ordered a twenty-eight. What is a seven- and-seven anyway—some kind of martini?

Ease

It's Seagram's Seven and Seven Up or sometimes Sprite.

Frieze

(To the inattentive bartender.) Scratch that last order, barkeep. Make it one seven-and- seven and one Scotch rocks—single malt.

Ease

Boy, you weren't kidding about not being a social expert. I'm not in any hurry.

Frieze

What do you mean?

Ease

I mean he looks kind of busy.

Frieze

The bartender? It's the middle of the day; the place is empty.

Ease

It looks like he's doing some paperwork.

Frieze

Paperwork? He's a bartender. His job is to take orders and make drinks. Bartenders are as overrated as newscasters and real estate agents.

Ease

And what's your job?

Frieze

I haven't got one.

Ease

Maybe until you get one you should lay off those that do.

Frieze

I've offended you somehow?

Ease

No, but you haven't bothered to ask myname.

Frieze

What can that possibly matter?

Ease

It matters to me.

Frieze

In that case I apologize. So what's your name then?

Ease

My name is Geoff, with a G, but people call me Ease.

Frieze

Then I shall call you Ease as well. It's much more interesting than Geoff with a G.

Ease

What's your name?

Frieze

I once too had a sobriquet. The people who knew me here called me Frieze.

Ease

How is it that you don't have a job, Frieze?

Frieze

I'm a writer—easy work if you can get it. I haven't published anything in years though.

Ease

What do you write—books, like Stephen King?

Frieze

Books, yes. Like Stephen King, no.

Ease

Do you know him?

Frieze

No, I never met him.

Ease

That's too bad, he's got talent. What are the names of the books you wrote?

Frieze

I've actually only published one. It was entitled *The Turning*.

Ease

I don't think I heard of it. Was it a mystery?

Frieze

No. It was a paperback with an orange cover.

Ease

That don't help none. I bet lots of books have…hold on, was it just an orange cover—no picture, no words on the outside?

Frieze

Yes, that's the one.

Ease

I know that book. Yeah, the title—

Frieze

And the author's name.

Ease

—was inside the cover. And every other page was printed upside down, so—

Frieze

So you could fold back the upside down pages. When you got to the last page you turned the book over and kept reading. It could be read from front to back and back again—a full-circle reading experience, or so the promos went.

Ease

I liked that one.

Frieze

So you read it then?

Ease

No, but I remember seeing it—thought it was a neat idea.

Frieze

It was my publisher's idea. He said the unconventional gim-
mick suited my unconventional writing style. He said no one
would ever forget that little orange book. I thought it was
asinine; besides, we could never do a hardcover edition.

Ease

So what was it like being famous?

Frieze

I was quasi-famous for about two months.

Ease

That's two more months than me and most other people. What
was it like?

Frieze

The Chrises from Connecticut were a real drag.

Ease

How's that?

Frieze

I'd get recognized at the most inopportune times, like right after
stuffing a fork-full of food into my mouth or a dead hooker

into my car trunk. And standing there would be a Chris from Connecticut, all ready to glad-hand me and tell me how inspirational they thought my book was. Don't misunderstand, I wasn't the cynic then that I am now. It was flattering, but I never had the knack for matching their enthusiasm. For the Chrises I was someone who got them—saw inside them. But to me, they were just Chris from Connecticut, who sold stationary or some such. How much enthusiasm could I be expected to muster about that? I'm a writer, not an actor. So these encounters inevitably resulted in the Chris's disappointment, leaving me feeling like anasshole.

Ease

Damn, that doesn't sound like any fun atall.

Frieze

To this day I can't walk into any stationary store in Connecticut.

Ease

Maybe I should write a book. I bet it ain't that hard.

Frieze

Sure, you could write one, but who's going to read it.

Ease

You'd be surprised. I've seen some shit that'd make you look sideways.

Frieze

I don't doubt that you have, but you miss my point. Anybody can write a book. I wrote a book a long time ago; then I wrote a stack of query letters ten feet tall. Never got so much as a postcard telling me to go fuck myself. Three years later I happen to date this girl, who happens to have an uncle, who happens to have a boyfriend, who happens to know some people in publishing, and in a few months I had a book deal. So what I'm saying is go ahead and write your book, and maybe it'll be tremendous, but unless you know someone with a gay uncle who has connections, I wouldn't quit your dayjob.

Ease

Maybe I could write the book, and then you could put your name on it, and we could split the profits.

Please

(Approaching with the seven-and-seven.) Here's your seven-and-seven. (Serving it to Ease and then turning to Frieze.) Yours will take a few more minutes. Oh, and say please, not barkeep.

Frieze

A few more minutes? All you have to do is pour some whiskey over ice.

Please

All my ice melted. I'm making more.

Frieze

But his has ice. (Indicating Ease's drink.)

Please

So it does. (He turns and walks back to the bar.)

Ease

See, you should be nicer.

Frieze

Perhaps you're onto something: Exploit unto others as you would have them exploit unto you

Scene II

(A dark prison cell. Frieze is the only occupant. He sits in a spotlight. The Steward and the Nutritionist are always in the shadows.)

Steward

Have you been level-two Mirandized yet?

Frieze

(Disoriented as if waking.) What? I don't know what you're saying. Where the hell am I? What is this place?

Steward

I thought not. (Reading.) You have the right to occupy this cell for as long as you so choose. You have the right to eat or not eat the food provided to you. You have the right to know that all provided food will be dosed with an odorless, tasteless, and painless lethal poison. You have the right to privacy for the term of your final reflection. You will have only verbal contact with your steward and your nutritionist. You will have physical contact with no one. You have the right to maintain your cell however you wish. It will not be disturbed until after you expire. Do you understand your rights?

Frieze

Who the fuck are you?

Steward

I am your steward. Your nutritionist will be along shortly.

Frieze

Who do you think I am? Because I'm not him.

Steward

Of course you are.

Frieze

Then tell me my name.

Steward

Your name is #655321. I will return to check on you tomorrow.

Frieze

Wait. Why am I here? Steward. Steward! (Time goes by.)

Nutritionist

Hello. I am your nutritionist, and I'm here to discuss your first and, if you so choose, last meal.

Frieze

You've got to get me out of here. There's been some sort of fuck up.

Nutritionist

Let's start with beverages. The first meal is always a breakfast. How about coffee and orange juice—I squeeze it fresh myself?

Frieze

What? No. You're not listening. I'm not supposed to be here!

Nutritionist

I can bring you a little rum with breakfast, if that will help calm your nerves.

Frieze

Just let me contact someone. Get me a line to the outside—now!

Nutritionist

Would you prefer a Belgium waffle, French toast, or an English muffin? I'll share a little secret with you. I've been at this for a long time, and the English muffin is by far our least popular European breakfast bread.

Frieze

You don't understand. You've got the wrong guy.

Nutritionist

Would you prefer bacon or sausage, though you're entitled to both if you wish? There aren't many vegetarians in here.

Frieze

Do you care at all?

Nutritionist

Of course I care. That's why I do this work—to make your remaining time as comfortable as possible. Now, how would you like your eggs?

Scene III

(Twenty years before in the same bar.)

Sleaze

Frieze invited me to this party. I think he's such a talented writer. It's like he can see right through you.

Louise

Of course you were invited to his party. You work for his publisher, who's throwing this party, which you organized.

Sleaze

What are you trying to say, Louise?

Louise

Just be careful with that one is all. He has a nasty habit of making you feel like the whole world one day and then like the least important person on it the next.

Sleaze

I don't think that's going to happen with us. We've made a real connection over the past few weeks. We even have our own nicknames for each other.

Louise

Really, you've already fallen for him?

Sleaze

The night we met he played me Carole King on his piano and taught me about wine. I couldn't help myself.

Cheese

(Cheese and Wheeze talking together.) So I understand congratulations are in order—a welcome addition.

Wheeze

Yes thank you.

Frieze

(Approaching.) A new book in your McGuffin series so soon? When do you find time to sleep?

Wheeze

No, no—Louise and I are pregnant.

Frieze

The both of you at the same time—that's quite a coincidence.

Cheese

I think our dear Frieze is making sport of your sensitive syntax.

Wheeze

A tune which is very familiar to me.

Frieze

Really, congratulations. I knew she'd find the right guy to settle down with eventually. It just goes to show you that looks aren't everything. Excuse me. (Moves to talk with Sleaze and Louise.)

Cheese

Off to the fox hunt. I think he's been aiming down the barrel of his prick at my new assistant. Even with all his talent, I believe she could do better.

Sleaze

(Frieze approaches Sleaze and Louise.) Oh, hello there.

Frieze

(Dismissively.) Yeah. (To Louise.) I need to talk to you. (Pulling Louise by the arm.) So it mine?

Louise

You can't be serious.

Frieze

You're pro-abortion.

Louise

I'm pro-choice, and what difference does that make?

Frieze

The difference is just get rid of it.

Louise

Why would I do that? I love him, and we're getting married.

Frieze

We could still have something.

Louise

I don't want anything with you.

Frieze

Then have the baby and give it up for adoption; I don't care. What kind of life are you going to have with him—a house in the sticks and a yard full of kids?

Louise

Go away. (Frieze stays but is silent. Sleaze moves to talk with Geeze who is sitting alone at the bar, nursing a glass of club soda.)

Geeze

You look troubled my dear. What's the matter?

Sleaze

I just found out that something I thought I had I really don't have at all.

Geeze

I've been having the opposite problem of late. I remember running out of cat food three weeks ago, but thrice since then I could not recall buying more. Now I have enough cat food to feed Mister Fritzgerald for a year. I think he's considering having me committed to the pound.

Sleaze

I guess we all have our problems.

Geeze

I should say so. I used to have a memory like…oh, you know… one of those large animals with the long noses.

Sleaze

Stop, you'll make me laugh, and I don't want to laugh because I'm sad. I can't handle more than one emotion right now.

Geeze

A young person like you—what have you got to be sad about? Wait until you're as old as me, and all this will seem like the time of your life. Tonight has been something of a triumph for you. You've thrown the best party this place has ever seen.

Sleaze

Really, you think the party is going well?

Geeze

Sure, people showed up for a change. I don't think we've ever had catering here before. And you made sure I kept the genie in the bottle.

Sleaze

Cheese said I should keep an eye on you.

Geeze

He was right to say so. In the past I too often ignored the inexorable fact that as my years advance my limits retreat. So now I sit before you, a reformed man, sipping club soda, while all the real drinking is happening at the blind pig in the backroom.

Frieze

(Approaches Sleaze and Geeze after Louise exits.) Sleaze, I need to get out of here. Get your coat.

Sleaze

I'm not going anywhere with you. And stop calling me that. It's not funny anymore. (Exits the bar.)

Frieze

There goes another one. They can be a real pain in the ass.

Geeze

Women? They're the most interesting of all God's creatures.

Frieze

Then they ought to be kept in zoos.

Geeze

It doesn't seem right that you should be so troubled at a party thrown in your honor. But it is necessary I'm afraid. No artist should go untortured lest their art suffer.

Frieze

Women are like penises. The one I've got is hardly worth the trouble, but then I can't help wondering what it'd be like to have another. How did you deal with them in your day, the broads I mean, after *The Dancer* was published?

Geeze

Broads—I haven't heard women called that in a long time. You've made an old man smile; however, you should be cautious when seeking counsel from a geezer like me. It's akin to asking a taxidermist to examine your W-2s.

Frieze

I probably won't listen much anyway—stories from World War II always bore me. Tell me how it was when people read? When books actually mattered.

Geeze

Oh, it wasn't all that different. Mostly what was read were newspapers and racing forms, and that's only because there was no television.

Frieze

I really thought when I got the career part of my life in order the rest would fall into place. Maybe I should just get married to simplify my life.

Geeze

You're too bright to have such a dim notion. Don't forget that men and women mostly want the same things, perhaps just in slightly different orders.

Frieze

You're right, of course; I am very bright. Did you think of that taxidermist doing your taxes bit just now?

Geeze

It's a line from a new book I'm writing. I haven't quite worked out the wording yet.

Frieze

It's a relief to know that I'm not the only one who self-plagiarizes at parties.

Geeze

If not for self-plagiarism, I'd hardly have anything at all of interest to say.

Frieze

Me too. I didn't know you were still writing.

Geeze

I've been putting the final touches on my new one for about two decades. How is your writing these days? Can we expect an imminent follow up to your first offering?

Frieze

I've been working on something. I'm thinking of entitling it *Perspicuous Perspicacity.*

Geeze

That's horrible. No one wants to buy a book with a title they don't understand; you need something more demotic—think *Slaughterhouse Five* not *Abattoir Five*. *The Turning* is a good title—gets to the crux of the matter.

Frieze

What crux? There's no crux. It doesn't mean anything. Calling it that was Cheese's idea.

Geeze

And a good idea it was. He hasn't become the publisher he is today without learning some things. Follow his advice and you'll enjoy a long career in this profession.

Frieze

I'm not even sure I want that.

Geeze

Try being a bartender, serving dyspeptic drunks for forty years like my brother, and then talk to me about what you want. He died on his feet behind the bar, never even fell over.

Frieze

What are you trying to tell me?

Geeze

I'm telling you that you should enjoy your moment while it lasts. Wear the crown with care. It's heavier than you think, and will slip sooner than you realize. But then the only thing easier than giving advice is giving bad advice, and the hardest thing of all might be understanding the difference.

ACT TWO

Scene I (tavern today)

Frieze

(Frieze and Ease are seated at the table, embroiled in a highly cerebral conversation.) No, no, no. *Temple of Doom* was released after *Raiders of the Lost Ark,* but the actual plot occurred before.

Ease

Well that's confusing.

Frieze

I'll grant you that. Did you know that *Temple of Doom* was the first movie to be rated PG-13?

Ease

Did you know that you never outright agree with me? You just say: I'll grant you that.

Wheeze

(Entering. Moving behind the bar and talking with the bartender. Then noticing Frieze.) Frieze, is that you?

Frieze

Wheeze? What the hell are you doing behind the bar?

Wheeze

(Approaching Frieze.) This is my place now. I own it.

Frieze

So the writing didn't work out after all?

Wheeze

You don't see many current movies?

Frieze

I mostly just watch old stuff—back when movies were about something.

Wheeze

I switched to screenwriting—less control, but more money. I even have a McGuffin script in preproduction.

Frieze

So you write the scripts and forgo the novels all together. How very efficient.

Wheeze

It is actually. And I like the process: author, actor, audience.

Frieze

Past, present, future.

Wheeze

Sure, I guess. This place is sort of a hobby of mine. I've had a lot of good times here. What's it been...like nineteen odd years since I've seen you?

Frieze

Nope, more like twenty even ones. Last time we spoke you and Louise were expecting. I was sorry to hear that she'd passed.

Wheeze

It was a tough time, losing her just after our son was born, but thankfully I had friends who helped me through. Anyway, it was a long time ago.

Frieze

How's your kid?

Wheeze

He's real good. He goes to school at the Art Institute.

Frieze

Learning how to paint with his own feces and the like?

Wheeze

No, no they supply the feces. You know, it's starting to come back to me why we didn't keep in touch. Are you still writing? I haven't heard Cheese mention your name in years.

Frieze

I've been working on some things.

Wheeze

How's the sell-through rate on your book these days?

Frieze

I have no idea. Twice a year they send me a check, and each time the amount is a little less than the time before.

Wheeze

Well it's refreshing to know that you don't keep tabs on your numbers. Most of my writer friends spend more time checking their Amazon ranking than actually writing. If you ever needed to, I'm sure you could still sell the film rights to your book.

Frieze

If one morning I wake up to a ringing phone, and it's my accountant calling to say that the money is all gone, then after I hang up, the phone rings again, and this time it's my doctor calling to say that I have a terminal illness whose only cure is a treatment that costs a million dollars, then after I hang up, the phone rings yet again, and this time it's some fuck-shit filmmaker calling to say that he'd pay a million dollars for the movie rights to my book—well, I'd tell him to go suck a dead man's cock.

Wheeze

It's nice to know that some things never change.

Ease

You mean he's always been this way?

Wheeze

For as long as I've known him.

Frieze

Wheeze, I'd like you to meet Ease.

Ease

(Shaking hands with Wheeze.) Good to meet you.

Wheeze

You too. I don't think I've seen you in here before?

Ease

My first time. It's a real nice place.

Wheeze

Thanks.

Frieze

I was telling Ease that it looks just the way it did twenty years ago.

Wheeze

That's the allure for me. It'll never change. The outside world is mutable, but this place will remain the same. When I first took ownership I had duplicates ordered of all the furniture and fixtures, so when anything gets worn out I can just replace it. It's all stored in the backroom. There's an entire replacement bar back there.

Frieze

That sounds insane.

Wheeze

One man's crazy is another man's sanity. I've got some things to do, but I'll be back in a bit. (Moving to the backroom and talking to the bartender.) Put those two drinks on the house. Let's go over yesterday's receipts when you get a chance. (Two exit to theback.)

Ease

He seems like a good guy.

Frieze

He's a pompous ass.

Ease

So he's a writer like you?

Frieze

Not like me. The difference between us is like the difference between an academic and an intellectual—one's a vocation, the other is a way of life.

Ease

I don't follow.

Frieze

He's a man not burdened by a great deal of talent. To say it plain, he's a hack. I'm certain there must be a kinder way of putting it, but none that would be more accurate.

Ease

I hate to think what you'll say about me after we part ways.

Frieze

Don't worry, I doubt I'll talk about you at all. So what's your line of work?

Ease

I'm a spare-changer.

Frieze

As in tires?

Ease

As in panhandling.

Frieze

You don't look like a street person.

Ease

These aren't my work clothes, and I don't live on the streets anymore. I have a room at the men's hotel not too far from here.

Frieze

Is it a nice place?

Ease

Beats sleeping under a bridge.

Frieze

So you can really make a living begging for change?

Ease

If you budget yourself, but sometimes the ends don't meet, and a body has to get creative.

Frieze

How so?

Ease

You ever punched a guy in the face before?

Frieze

You mean physically?

Ease

How else is there?

Frieze

No, I've never punched anyone in the face.

Ease

Neither have most guys, but it's something just about every dude wants to try once in his life.

Frieze

So you let people punch you in the face for money?

Ease

When times are tight.

Frieze

How much do you charge?

Ease

Usually forty. I give twenty back if they can knock me down, but it hasn't happened yet—knock wood. (Ease knocks on his head.)

Frieze

And you've never had your jaw broken?

Ease

Nah, you just gotta know when to turn your chin and roll with the punch.

Frieze

Is that why your eye is that way—the one that doesn't ever seem to be looking in the right direction?

Ease

Yeah, I got my sock orbit fractured once.

Frieze

Orbital socket—you should get that checked out. It could become a problem if there are still bone fragments floating around in there.

Ease

It got that way a long time ago. If something was going to happen, it would've happened by now. Besides, I'm letting people punch me in the face for money, it's not like I have cash for a doctor.

Sleaze

(Enters, walks up to the bar, looks around, and asks rhetorically.) What does a person have to do to get a drink in here?

Frieze

(Not realizing who it is.) You get the pellets from the pellet dispenser, who just stepped into the backroom.

Sleaze

(Recognizing Frieze.) Is…is that you?

Frieze

That's a matter of perspective.

Sleaze

What are you doing here? It's been years.

Frieze

(Realizing who it is.) Oh, I'm so sorry. I didn't recognize you.

Sleaze

What are you doing here? I haven't seen you in—

Frieze

Years. Yes, it's been a long time. I apologize. (Uncertain of what to say.) I saw Wheeze a minute ago. He's in the backroom. This is Ease.

Ease

Nice to meet you.

Sleaze

(Focusing on Frieze.) What are you doing here?

Frieze

I thought I'd come back for, hell I don't know, old-time's sake. I'll be leaving soon, and—

Sleaze

I thought you'd left a long time ago.

Frieze

I did, but then I came back.

Sleaze

And you never called any of us? You never called me.

Frieze

You know how I feel about phones, and I didn't really see the point. I'm not sure what good would've come from it.

Sleaze

But you're here now, as if this were still your usual place?

Frieze

I have fond memories of this bar—some of them with you. It hasn't changed at all, has it?

Sleaze

The people have. (Exits to the backroom.)

Ease

Man, you must've done something to really piss her off.

Frieze

I once told her that I wanted to crash my fuselage into her cockpit.

Ease

(Sarcastically.) Classy. What'd she do?

Frieze

Married me. Then filed for divorce a year later, but some things happened in between.

Ease

You've got a real special way with people.

Frieze

I've been careless with people who cared for me.

Scene II
(Back in prison.)

Frieze

(Hearing someone enter.) Is that you steward?

Nutritionist

(Still unseen.) No, it's your nutritionist, here to go over the day's menu—a lunch this time. I see from your non-dead state that yesterday's breakfast was not to your liking.

Frieze

The meal was as unwelcome as your humor. You know I shouldn't be here.

Nutritionist

Of course you should.

Frieze

Why?

Nutritionist

Because you broke the law.

Frieze

What law did I break?

Nutritionist

Failure to show remorse.

Frieze

How can I show remorse when I don't even know what it is that I'm supposed to be be remorseful about?

Nutritionist

That's it precisely. Only someone without remorse wouldn't be able to identify the reason for which they should beremorseful.

Frieze

So you're fucking with me, is that it? My death is just a joke.

Nutritionist

I know it can be unpleasant here. I'm doing the best I can for you. I genuinely want your last meal to be the most delectable you've ever had.

Frieze

What's the longest someone has lasted in here?

Nutritionist

There was a guest of ours that made it six days.

Frieze

Did he die of thirst? Starve?

Nutritionist

No, his throat swelled shut from his constant screaming, and he choked to death.

Frieze

You won't hear me scream like that.

Nutritionist

There was another fellow, this was before my time, that lasted almost two weeks, but he cheated a little. He gnawed at his wrists and drank his own blood.

Frieze

So he bled to death?

Nutritionist

No, his stomach burst. It seems drinking too much blood can kill you.

Frieze

Quite the thanatology lab you have here. How long do most people last?

Nutritionist

Three days. How about a Cuban sandwich for your next meal? Slow-roasted pork loin, smoky Swiss cheese, honey-cured pro- sciutto, and a smear of stone-ground mustard, a proprietary blend, all pressed and toasted on a ciabatta roll—with some salty shoe-string fries on the side and a big bottle of lager to wash it down, or a cider if you prefer.

Frieze

I don't care. I'm not eating it.

Nutritionist

I'll make it anyway, in case you find your appetite.

Frieze

Wait.

Nutritionist

Yes?

Frieze

So all the food is poisoned?

Nutritionist

Yes, but I assure you it doesn't affect the taste. After your meal, you simply fall asleep and never wake up—quite relaxing I'm told.

Frieze

But the beer, does it come in an unopened bottle.

Nutritionist

Of course, to maintain freshness.

Frieze

So then it's not poisoned.

Nutritionist

They dose it at the brewery.

Scene III

(Twenty years and a month before in the same bar. Louise and Frieze sit alone at a table in the otherwise empty bar.)

Frieze

You're a slimy cunt.

Louise

And you're a vindictive misanthrope.

Frieze

I'm offering you everything that you said you wanted a few months ago. Why are you saying no?

Louise

Why did you leave? You didn't even tell me you were going. I had to find out from Cheese that you'd left the city, and he didn't know where you'd gone or if you were coming back.

Frieze

I had to get away to figure some things out about my novel and about us, but I'm back now, and I know I want you, so let's go away together.

Louise

Your answer to everything is to just go away. Don't you see how damaging that can be? Women can't always just leave a situation when it suits us. Sometimes we get stuck.

Frieze

Stop being this way. You act like you're playing a character from one of Wheeze's awful books.

Louise

Maybe it's not the characters you object to; maybe it's their happy endings.

Frieze

I object to all of it: the happy endings, the inane dialogue, the ludicrous plots. There isn't a micron of authenticity in any of it.

Louise

Who are you to question anyone's authenticity? I've never heard you once express a genuine, unburnished sentiment. Wheeze writes about the way he wants the world to be.

Frieze

And I see the world as it is.

Louise

Maybe that's not the gift you think it is. All you see are shadows. Maybe you're jealous that he can see the light too.

Frieze

How can I be jealous of someone who doesn't have anything that I want? Why the hell are we talking about Wheeze anyway?

Louise

He asked me to marry him, and I said yes.

Frieze

That's ridiculous.

Louise

Why is it ridiculous?

Frieze

It's ridiculous because you're marrying him to get back at me for leaving when I'm right here in front of you. Now who's being vindictive?

Louise

I made a promise to him.

Frieze

You're engaged. That's a promise to make a promise—not the same thing.

Louise

He's a good man, and you aren't.

Frieze

What's that got to do with anything? You love me, and I love you in a way that he never could.

Louise

You think you're capable of such incredible insight, but all you ever do with your so-called powers of perception is run everybody down. You can't see that you're walking on the bottom of the ocean.

Frieze

What are you on about now? I'm not sure I can handle another of your silly metaphors.

Louise

You're not spiraling downward; you sank a long time ago. You only think you're looking down on all of us because your arrogant self-delusion has flipped your perspective.

Frieze

I'm sure you've spent these past months thinking of all the nasty things you would say to me for leaving without a goodbye, but let's—

Louise

No, when you asked to meet me here I didn't know what I would say...I didn't know what you would say. There were weeks that went by when I'd hoped you'd suddenly show up, but now that I see you sitting here it's so clear to me.

Frieze

And what is it that's so clear?

Louise

I do care about you, and I wish you a good life, but I can't be with you.

Frieze

Why?

Louise

Because you're a miserable person who brings misery into the lives of everyone you know. I'm not sure if the world made you this way or if it's just the way you are, and it really doesn't matter. I don't want to waste the rest of my life with you on the ocean floor. (Rising to leave.)

Frieze

Stay and help me be a better man. (Grabbing for her hand.)

Louise

I can't…I can't see you anymore. (Exits.)

Frieze

She lectures me for leaving and then leaves herself. (Frieze drinks his drink and then he yells for the bartender, not realizing that he is alone.) Barkeep, bring me another. (Frieze moves behind the bar and takes a shot.) I hope her marriage kills her. (Takes another shot. Contemplative now.) I don't wish she was dead; I wish she never was. (Becoming aware of his drunkenness.) Who am I talking to? (Sleaze enters disheveled.) Has it started to stormyet?

Sleaze

(Sitting at the bar.) I don't know.

Frieze

You just came in from outside. How can you not know?

Sleaze

What are you, a bartender or a weatherman?

Frieze

Neither. But it looks like you could use a drink. What'll you have?

Sleaze

What you're having. Do they let bartenders drink on the job?

Frieze

(Pouring them both a shot.) Not as a rule, but like I said I'm not the bartender.

Sleaze

No, I know who you are. My boss represents you, doesn't he? You're one of his writers.

Frieze

Yes, Cheese is my publisher.

Sleaze

It's funny that you call him that. I saw you in the office the other day. I didn't recognize you out of context.

Frieze

And your Cheese's new girl Friday.

Sleaze

What's that supposed to mean?

Frieze

That you're his assistant.

Sleaze

Oh, then yes I am. I thought you were trying to say something creepy. Not that I think you're creepy or anything.

Frieze

Sure you do. There's no reason for us to have secrets.

Sleaze

So you are a little creepy then?

Frieze

More than a little. But you're seventeen years old. You think anyone who doesn't look as if they should be on television is creepy, even though they're usually the biggest creeps.

Sleaze

I'm twenty-three.

Frieze

Then I thought you would've figured that out by now. So do you want to tell me about it?

Sleaze

About what?

Frieze

You look like you've had a rough night.

Sleaze

I just got dumped by this crappy guy.

Frieze

It sounds like he did you a favor. How long had you been seeing this crappy guy?

Sleaze

Three weeks.

Frieze

That's not even a month.

Sleaze

So?

Frieze

So, you're not allowed be upset about a relationship that lasted less than a month. It's a rule.

Sleaze

Whose rule?

Frieze

Everyone's. It's a universal rule; one might even say it's axiomatic.

Sleaze

That's dumb. Anyway, I'm not crying over him.

Frieze

So why the tears?

Sleaze

I don't know. Ever since I moved here my social life has been really pathetic—a string of relationships that never last more than a few weeks.

Frieze

That sounds like a rather successful social life to me, though I can't help thinking there is more to this story.

Sleaze

The bastard photographed me naked. Things were going really well with us and I trusted him. He bought one of those Polaroid cameras and thought it might be fun to take some nude pictures. I just found out he's been showing the photos to his friends, and now I feel like some sleazy whore. What's wrong with me?

Frieze

To begin with, Sleaze, you're being too hard on yourself. It's tough to live in a new place. Hell, it's tough being twenty-three. As for these Polaroids, your generation isn't to blame.

Sleaze

How's that?

Frieze

Did your parents ever take pictures of you as a child—photograph your first birthday, your first steps?

Sleaze

Sure.

Frieze

Then there you have it. Your generation was raised in front of the camera, with your mother photographing every dance recital and your father shooting pics of every basketball game, it's only natural that you'd consent to some naughty Polaroids—the final images of your journey to adulthood. When you think about it, it's rather tidy how childhood is bookended by vaginal extraction and insertion.

Sleaze

That's gross…and it wasn't my first time or anything, but you make a good point.

Frieze

My head's floating in so much bourbon, I'm surprised I make any sense at all. (Pouring two more shots.) So why did you come here tonight?

Sleaze

I didn't have any place else to go. I hardly know my way around yet. I only knew this place because I've been making arrangements for some lame book release party here in a few weeks.

Frieze

I hope that isn't what you put on the invitations.

Sleaze

The party's not for your…oh, it is. I'm so—

Frieze

Don't be. I'm sure your description will prove most prescient.

Sleaze

It'll be so lame that it's crippled.

Frieze

What a droll thing to say. Sleaze, we should leave here at once?

Sleaze

Where would we go, Creepy?

Frieze

I have a piano at my place, and I know an amusing anecdote about an aviation mishap.

Sleaze

Can I trust you?

Frieze

Not at all, but I can assure you that I don't own a camera of any kind. (The two exit together.)

ACT THREE

Scene I

(Frieze and Ease are still seated at the table.)

Ease

(Finishing his drink.) You still buying?

Frieze

Sure. Another mixed drink?

Ease

I've never had champagne before. I think I'll try that.

Frieze

You've never had a champagne cocktail?

Ease

I've had fizzy wine before, but never champagne. Is a champagne cocktail different from a regular glass of champagne?

Frieze

Champagne is a region in France, so unless the wine is made there it can't accurately be called champagne—like bourbon is to Kentucky or Scotch is to Scotland. A lesson in cultural topography one libation at a time.

Ease

That's not what I asked.

Frieze

What did you ask?

Ease

How is a champagne cocktail different from a glass of champagne?

Frieze

There is no difference; they are one and the same.

Ease

Then why's it got two names? Why not just order a glass of champagne?

Frieze

You might as well ask why people say laconic instead of terse or reticent instead of taciturn?

Ease

What do those words mean?

Frieze

They're similar to the opposite of loquacious…or garrulous… or effusive.

Ease

I have no idea what you're talking about now. All I want to know is why I have to order a champagne cocktail when what I want is a glass of champagne.

Frieze

Because that is the system we've chosen. Why do we feel compelled to say hello when we answer the phone? Why not rather
say pumpkin or hippopotamus? The meaning would be the
same if everyone decided it should be so. Why do we say bless
you when people sneeze, but nothing at all when they cough
or hiccup? Wouldn't it be a comfort to say I hope your hic-
cups burn in hell? These are the rules, for better or for worse,
whether they make sense or not. One day, long from now,
people will speak in numbers. Instead of good morning, they'll
say three. Instead of pardon me, they'll say forty-six. Then after
that there won't be any talking at all, and that's when people
will really start to communicate.

Ease

I didn't choose this system. I was born into it, and I have no
choice about it.

Frieze

What you say is only half true. You always have the choice not
to live in the system.

Please

(Approaching.) You need another round?

Frieze

Another Scotch rocks for me, and a ninety-two for him.

Ease

He means can I get a champagne cocktail?

Please

You want that with the sugar cube, bitters, and cherry garnish?

Ease

No, I just want a glass of champagne.

Please

I thought so. It's a common mistake. (Returns to the bar.)

Ease

I guess you don't know everything.

Frieze

So I might not make the world's best bartender. I'll add that to the list of jobs I never wanted in the first place. What compelled you to order champagne anyway? It's only a Tuesday.

Ease

People drink champagne on Ney Year's Eve, and those can fall on a Tuesday.

Frieze

Yes, but they order champagne then because it's New Year's Eve—not because it's Tuesday. You drink champagne at a celebration because the bubbles are convivial. You drink vodka at a funeral and on an international flight because the journey is long. You drink beer at a baseball game because the sun is hot. You drink rye around a campfire because the night is cold. You drink red wine with steak because the blood is runny. You drink white wine with fish because the mercury is bitter. You drink rum on an island because the ocean is salty. You drink tequila in a desert because the water is precious. You drink Scotch with strangers because they might know you better than you think. And you drink gin alone because you are your own best company.

Ease

I bet you were a good writer. How come it's been so long since you've written a book?

Frieze

If I had to hazard a guess, I suppose it's because I haven't got anything interesting left to say—perhaps I never did and only came to realize it later in life.

Ease

So you don't think you'll ever write anything again?

Frieze

I once had a short story published; it was entitled *Mysolation*. The journal that published it paid me in postage stamps—six of them I believe it was. I was over the moon; after all, six is twice as many as three. By the time my novel was finally published, it had been through so much editing that I didn't recognize it anymore, and I was sure it was doomed to fail. But instead my book by committee became a modest success and then an immense one. I doubt... rather I know if my book had been published the way it was first written it would've slipped away unread, and I too would have disappeared...unwanted. I could write another one—let them turn half the pages upside down again and hell maybe even make the cover transparent this time. It would probably sell very well.

Ease

So why don't you?

Frieze

Because as terrible as it is to want only one thing in this world and never get it, I promise you it is far worse to get that one thing and then have it cut away from you.

Ease

As usual I have no idea what you're talking about.

Frieze

(Laughs a little.) It's like playing Yahtzee without the dice—perhaps it's ineffable. Let's just say that the indifference of the world has diminished my capacity to give a shit and leave it at that.

Wheeze

(Approaching from the backroom and then the bar with a Scotch and Ease's glass of Champagne.) Sounds like you could use another drink.

Frieze

Thanks. Where is Sleaze?

Wheeze

My wife will be out in a moment. It was quite a surprise for her to see you here after all these years. And do me the courtesy of not calling her—

Frieze

Of course, old habit, sorry. I didn't know you two were together.

Wheeze

She didn't take your divorce well, and I lost Louise around the same time. We found a connection in our misery you might say. We dated off and on and then finally married. Our ten year anniversary is in a couple of months.

Frieze

I didn't realize she was so troubled by our divorce. We were married such a short time; it was all a lark really.

Wheeze

It was more than that to her.

Frieze

I'm glad you were there for her.

Wheeze

We were there for each other. I thought I'd never get over losing Louise, and I never have, but together we were able to share the parts that the other had lost.

Frieze

It's good that you two have one another. I suppose that you and I share more than just history.

Wheeze

Of course Louise told me of you two.

Frieze

I'm sorry, but it was a long time ago.

Wheeze

Yes it was. I'm thankful for every moment I had with her—the good and the bad.

Frieze

At least you have someone now. I haven't got anyone. Isn't it peculiar how it all works? I mean the whole thing: love and loss, misery and ecstasy, sex and the supernatural; every beautiful thing is tied to something ugly, and in that balance we find faith in our godless universe. (Examining his drink.) It's like a cosmic storm brewing between the ice cubes.

Wheeze

Maybe. I'll leave it for you to decide; you always were the metaphysician. (Turning to Ease.) Forgive us, we just needed to do a bit of catching up. So what's your field?

Ease

I guess you could say I'm in the field of begging.

Wheeze

Most of the writers I know are beggars—it's honest work. (To the bartender again.) When they're ready bring our guests another round on the cuff.

Frieze

I am quite capable of paying for our drinks.

Wheeze

I'm sure you are, but it's my pleasure.

Ease

We appreciate it. I guess not all writers need to beg. You two seem to have made out pretty good.

Wheeze

I was fortunate to find a devoted audience. I'd publish a new volume in my McGuffin series every other Christmas. It was a grind, but a good grind, though I never enjoyed the meteoric success that Frieze had.

Frieze

You've had the same amount of success; it's just been spread over a longer period of time, and I'm not sure it isn't better that way.

Ease

(To the emerging Sleaze.) Oh, hello.

Sleaze

I'm sorry if I was rude before. (Extending her hand to Ease.) What is your name?

Ease

People call me Ease.

Frieze

He's a friend of mine.

Sleaze

Then he must not know you very well. (To Ease.) It is good to meet you.

Frieze

The old me would've rejoined with something like: you've lost your looks but found your tongue.

Sleaze

You are the old you, and now I too am old.

Wheeze

You're still as beautiful as ever.

Frieze

You were lovelier when I saw you last, but your husband is right to say that you are beautiful still.

Sleaze

Thank you both.

Frieze

I must be your foil, Wheeze. Women find in you what they don't in me, making you look better by comparison.

Sleaze

Yes, you two do contrast rather well, like a dead person and one who isn't.

Frieze

There you go being clever again. You were never so clever when I knew you.

Sleaze

Perhaps you just didn't bother to see it.

Ease

Do you people always talk this way?

Wheeze

I'm afraid so. We writers have the poor manners of too often speaking our minds. (To Frieze.) My darling has become something of a writer herself. She and Cheese have been conspiring over a manuscript of hers for some months now and are looking to publish it next year.

Frieze

Is it any good?

Wheeze

I'm sure it is, though neither of them has let me see a word of it.

Frieze

(To Sleaze.) A screed of dreadful poetry I imagine, as if there were any other kind.

Sleaze

A novel actually. Cheese says it's transcendent.

Frieze

The ramblings of an old man. He has to be in his mid-hundreds by now.

Sleaze

Wasn't it your mentor who once said, "The world is full of things you should read and nothing you shouldn't."

Frieze

Geeze was never my mentor, only my friend. (To Wheeze.) I saw the obituary you wrote for him.

Wheeze

I'm sure he would have preferred that it had been written by you. I sat with him in the hospice just before he died. He told me the trick to a good life was to be brave and kind. In his addled state, I think he thought he was talking to you. We looked for you at the funeral.

Frieze

I was out of the country then, I think.

Sleaze

So how have you been occupying your time since your return?

Frieze

By emitting and absorbing sound. I'm afraid that's all I'm good for these days.

Wheeze

Really, what have you been doing since we saw you last?

Frieze

Do you remember me nattering on about that drive-in movie theater of my youth—how I would while away my summer nights there?

Wheeze

I don't recall you mentioning that at all.

Sleaze

You said something to me about it...once.

Frieze

Really? Huh. Well I bought one.

Sleaze

You bought a drive-in theater?

Frieze

Out in Wyoming—right between a buffalo ranch and the middle of nowhere. It was one of those old-timey deals where the picture was projected on the broad-side of a narrow five-story building; each of its floors was six feet wide and fifty feet across. I lived there while I fixed the place up, took a whole year. It was the most exquisite thing you ever saw.

Wheeze

Are you joking?

Ease

I just met you, but it sounds like a joke to me.

Frieze

This was about ten years ago. I learned how to operate the projector, and I installed a sound system so people could listen to the movies through their car radios instead of those loathsome speakers on poles. It took me a week to cut all those poles down. I used a pipe cutter like Paul Newman with those parking meters in *Cool Hand Luke*.

Sleaze

So you actually opened this place to the public and...dealt with the public.

Frieze

Yes. Well no. I hired a husband and wife, an older Indian couple, to help me. She ran the concession stand, and he sold the tickets. I was the projectionist.

Ease

What were their names? Mr. and Mrs.Bull-Shit?

Frieze

I believe their surname is Silver-Cloud; they're Shoshone.

Wheeze

So what happened? Is the place still in business?

Frieze

We got off to a tremendous start. I only showed classic movies—nothing less than thirty years old. People drove in from all over. Then a few months after we opened a disabled girl was assaulted in our bathroom by two high school boys. No charges were pressed, so I burned the place to the ground. All that's left is the charred skeleton of a skinny building... and the buffalo.

Ease

I still can't tell if he's making it up.

Sleaze

No, he's telling the truth. He's always done exactly what he wants as long as it amuses him to do so and then gives up when things get complicated.

Frieze

So I'm an asshole because I think success is insidious?

Sleaze

No, you're an asshole because you always quit. You could've held a fundraiser for the girl's college education, or a film festival to raise awareness about violence against women, but you didn't. Instead you just gave up.

Frieze

Why don't you put all the things I should've done differently in that novel of yours—the memoir of your ephemeral and oppressive marriage to a has-been writer? I'm the only interesting thing that's ever happened to you.

Sleaze

You're the worst thing that's ever happened to me. I wondered what it would be like if I ever saw you again, but now that you're here I'm reminded of just how miserable a person you really are, and I sincerely hope this is the last time I ever see you. (Exits.)

Frieze

(Calling after her.) Be sure to remember me in your dedication.

Wheeze

You can be unforgivable. (Rises to leave.)

Frieze

Yes, yes. I'm sure I owe everyone I've ever met an apology. You'd better go after her. You two really are perfect for each other; you're full of shit and she's as plain as toilet paper.

Wheeze

(To the bartender.) This one has had enough. Please call him a cab. (Exits.)

Frieze

I make them run off, and he chases them down. (After a pause, to Ease.) Come on, let's go find somewhere else to drink.

Ease

The man didn't say I had to leave.

Frieze

So you're staying?

Ease

I like it here.

Frieze

Fine, all it will cost you is your own money. I need to make preparations for my departure anyhow.

Ease

Still leaving town, huh?

Frieze

That's correct.

Ease

People are sure going to miss you.

Frieze

Right. (Turns to leave, then pauses.) Oh, one last thing, Ease.

Ease

What's that?

Frieze

I've never punched anybody in the face.

Ease

I don't need the money today.

Frieze

And how about tomorrow?

Ease

I don't know, it ain't come yet.

Frieze

I'll pay you two hundred dollars.

Ease

They don't have people to punch where you're headed?

Frieze

Maybe they do, but I'm offering you five-times your going rate today.

Ease

My policy is to always get the money up front.

Frieze

That seems sensible enough. (Gives Ease two hundred dollars.) So I get a hundred back if I knock you down.

Ease

Sure, but like I told you that ain't never happened before.

Please

You can't do this in here.

Ease

(Preparing himself.) Relax, it'll be over before you know it.

Frieze

Ready?

Ease

Are you?

Frieze

(Winds up and throws his punch. Ease takes a step back as he rolls with it. Then Ease throws a punch, knocking Frieze to the floor. Frieze collects himself and rises to his feet.) What the fuck?

Ease

I always do that. I figure if you've never punched a guy in the face, then you probably never been punched in the face either. Don't worry, it ain't no extra charge. (Retakes his seat.)

Frieze

Give me back my money, you reprobate!

Ease

Why should I? You got to punch me in the face like we agreed. I didn't fall down, did I?

Frieze

You hitting me wasn't part of our agreement, and I don't give a damn about your obtuse, street-person logic.

Ease

You hit me, and I hit you back. There's nothing abstruse about it...even if I am a street person. But hey, if you're upset, I'll let you hit me again...for another two hundred dollars.

Frieze

This, right here, is the reason you haven't made anything of your pathetic life. I could've helped you. You'll remember me, but I will have forgotten all about you by tomorrow. By then I'll just be hungover, but you'll still be a lifetime loser.(Exits.)

Ease

(To the bartender.) Do you have anything to eat? I can pay. Please (Confused.) Sure, I'll find you something.

Scene II
(Back in prison.)

Frieze

Steward, where's the Nutritionist?

Steward

Why, do you plan on eating today?

Frieze

No, but I prefer his company to yours.

Steward

How come? He's the one trying to poison you.

Frieze

(Sarcastically.) Why are you always so funny?

Steward

Gallows humor helps the time pass quickly.

Frieze

Says you. My time here has been as torpid as that spent in any museum of modern art. Why hasn't the Nutritionist been by to take my order?

Steward

Today is your dinner meal. The Nutritionist never takes dinner orders. He always serves the same thing: meat and potatoes.

Frieze

That doesn't seem like much to turn down.

Steward

You haven't seen the cut of meat yet. You've never had a steak so good. The beef is aged on the premises.

Frieze

I had some damn good steaks on the outside.

Steward

Not like this. The smell alone will make you forget the name of the first girl you fell in love with.

Frieze

We'll see.

Steward

Only two percent of our residents make it past the dinner day.

Frieze

I'll wager my liberation from this immurement that I will be here and hungry tomorrow.

Steward

You have a funny way of talking. I bet you were somebody important on the outside.

Frieze

I was…a writer.

Steward

I guess that makes sense considering your crime.

Frieze

Eating myself to death is a senseless punishment for a crime that makes no sense.

Steward

Your victims probably thought your crimes were senseless too.

Frieze

This is all a farce—theater of the absurd.

Steward

I'm sure you were an imaginative writer. (Exits.)

Nutritionist

(Time passes. The Nutritionist can be heard entering. Serves a covered plate into the light but remains in the shadows.) Dinner is served.

Frieze

Where the hell have you been?

Nutritionist

I've been grilling your steak, roasting your potatoes, sautéing your asparagus, and decanting your claret.

Frieze

Asparagus? You think you can tempt me with asparagus?

Nutritionist

This asparagus was prepared using my own recipe, a house specialty.

Frieze

What's for dessert?

Nutritionist

A fortune cookie.

Frieze

A fortune cookie? That hardly seems appropriate for the meal.

Nutritionist

It's the fortune that is appropriate—not the vessel.

Frieze

What's it read?

Nutritionist

It's the only fortune that is always accurate, and one that I doubt any chef but me would dare to serve.

Frieze

Everyone dies.

Nutritionist

You're a very clever man. No matter how the cookie crumbles, that fortune will always be true.

Frieze

So let's have a look. (He reaches for the covered plate.)

Nutritionist

I must insist that you leave the dish covered until you are ready to dine, so as not to allow the aromas to escape before their time.

Frieze

Everything in its prison. (He withdraws his hand.) As a fellow artist, I will respect your wish. So what's the cut of beef?

Nutritionist

That depends. Where were you from?

Frieze

I've lived all over.

Nutritionist

Where did you order your first steak then?

Frieze

I'm not really sure…Chicago maybe.

Nutritionist

Hmm, then I don't know what cut of meat this would be to you.

Frieze

How can you not know?

Nutritionist

Well, if you'd said someplace back east then it'd be a New York strip, and if you'd said someplace out west then it'd be a Kansas City strip. But Illinois—that's right in the middle, isn't it? Sometimes naming a thing can be more trouble than it's worth.

Frieze

(Frieze laughs to himself.) Yes, nomenclature can be tedious.

Nutritionist

Indeed. I'll leave you to your dinner. I hope you enjoy it. (Exits.)

Frieze

Do you mean you hope I'll enjoy it or you hope I'll eat it and die? (He waits for a response, but he is alone.)

Scene III

(Twenty years and a few months before in the same bar. Wheeze and Louise are seated at the table with Geeze standing nearby.)

Frieze

(Entering with Cheese.) I'm sick of this place. Why do we always come here?

Cheese

I wouldn't know where else to throw one of these soirees. Besides, it's a tradition.

Frieze

Traditions are usually good things. This place is more like a bad habit.

Cheese

Come now. These are our colleagues.

Frieze

Where exactly are all of our colleagues? By my count the colleagues number precisely two and then some sort of other person with Wheeze there.

Cheese

Oh dear, you're right. Well, I'm sure the rest will be along later.

Frieze

Did you forget to invite our so-called colleagues—again?

Cheese

Of course not. After all, you're here.

Frieze

Because you picked me up, and it was a complete surprise when you knocked on my door.

Cheese

I really should hire someone to help me plan these events. Never mind that now, one of our own has had a success, and we should celebrate.

Frieze

It's the fourth book in his McGuffin series, and I'll be damned if I can tell one from the rest.

Cheese

Truth be told, they all sort of run together for me too. But his sales move steadily upwards. He's a career novelist, like you'll be one day with a bit of luck.

Frieze

You make it sound like a prison sentence.

Cheese

And remind me of your last, more liberated career?

Frieze

Yes, it is better to live in a prison with good grub than go hungry.

Cheese

I would've phrased it differently, but I quite agree. Let's get a drink before we congratulate the guest of honor.

Frieze

Let's make it a big one. (The two head for the untended bar.)

Wheeze

(To Geeze.) I know I'm not supposed to ask, but what do you think?

Geeze

Of your book or your beguiling lady friend?

Wheeze

My book of course. I value your opinion a great deal. *The Dancer* inspired me to become a writer.

Geeze

Pity it didn't inspire you to become a dancer. (Dances Louise out of her chair.)

Louise

(Playfully.) Why, I hardly know you, sir.

Wheeze

Well, Geeze?

Louise

Your interrogation is putting my new dance partner on the spot.

Geeze

A location to which I've become much accustomed to over the years. (To Wheeze.) I quite enjoy your pedantic prose; you have a knack for painting a meticulously detailed image. It's almost as if one can watch your books instead of read them.

Wheeze

Thank you Geeze. Your words are very kind, though I feel you have not said your whole piece. Any criticism you care to add to your compliment.

Geeze

I'm not sure I care to exactly, but since you ask: I feel the same about your novels as I do about the writing of most of your contemporaries—well rendered but not well wrought. I think it must be all that education your generation has. You spend so many years studying how to write but not what to write. Good writing can be learned, but I've never seen any evidence that it can be taught. It's not your fault of course; the culture has simply changed. Today one needs to be credentialed before one can be published.

Frieze

(Approaching with Cheese.) What are you going on about now Geeze, Social Security?

Wheeze

The venerable writing maestro was just chastising our generation's authors for being too…prosaic, would you say?

Louise

Style over substance.

Geeze

Yes that was the gist of it.

Frieze

An old, crotchety guy who thinks everything was better back in his day…I've got to tell you, Geeze, I didn't see that one coming.

Geeze

Ah, sarcasm: the wit of the witless.

Louise

(Annoyed by Frieze's rudeness.) And who are you?

Wheeze

He's another of Cheese's writers. We affectionately call him Frieze.

Frieze

(Giving a stiffly martial bow.) Ma'am, and what is your name?

Louise

Louise.

Frieze

That's a funny name.

Louise

You think my name is funny, do you Frieze?

Frieze

No, I just mean it's not a name you hear that often anymore.

Louise

So have you written anything I might've read?

Geeze

Not unless in addition to your great beauty you've been blessed with the ability to see into the future. We are awaiting our boy's debut novel with much anticipation.

Wheeze

How is it coming along?

Cheese

A few more slight changes. We're off to press in a month or so.

Louise

Is it any good?

Cheese

It's transcendent.

Frieze

It's ridiculous. I wrote the damn thing over three years ago. I don't even know what it's about anymore. And the cover treatment is absurd.

Cheese

We're doing something a bit unconventional with this one.

Wheeze

I'm anxious to see it. (To Cheese.) I've been after you to come up with a new direction for the covers of my last couple of books.

Geeze

New ideas beget new ideas.

Frieze

And what do old rummies beget?

Geeze

(Raising his empty glass.) Refills.

Frieze

(Moving toward the bar with Geeze.) I'd better chaperon to keep you from taking off your pants and trying to make us count the wrinkles.

Geeze

You'd do better to count the inches. You know it gets longer as you get older.

Frieze

That's an old-wives tale.

Geeze

Old wives ought to know.

Louise

(With Wheeze and Cheese.) Your friend is an impudent one.

Wheeze

He's always good for a laugh.

Cheese

He can be a handful. He's talented and he knows it. Soon he'll have moved beyond the need for praise or critique—in a realm unto himself.

Wheeze

Then how will you control him?

Cheese

The same way I control all you writers—with the promise of money.

Geeze

(Helping themselves behind the bar.) Where is the damned Scotch? Where is the damned bartender for that matter?

Frieze

Cheese made the arrangements, so he should be here soon or not at all.

Geeze

That explains the paucity of attendees. (Still looking for Scotch.)

Frieze

(Helping him look.) You didn't get an invitation then?

Geeze

No, I just happened to be walking by and saw that the place was open. When I came in it was empty except for Wheeze and his gal. He asked if I was here for his release party. I didn't have the heart to say no.

Frieze

I wonder who let them in? (Pointing to a bottle.) Isn't that Scotch over there?

Geeze

I don't want that blended shit.

Frieze

(Exasperated with the search.) Did you try looking for it up your ass then?

Geeze

No, but only because I'm afraid of what I might find in there. (Selecting a bottle and pouring himself a drink.) This will have to do. So what did you think of her?

Frieze

Her who?

Geeze

Her who indeed. I saw the way you looked at her.

Frieze

I talked to her for two minutes.

Geeze

An empire could've been built in those two minutes.

Frieze

I'd say Wheeze couldn't do any better for himself. Why go out for a hamburger when you've got a cow at home.

Geeze

(Starting to slur his words.) The laddie doth protest too much, methinks.

Frieze

And methinks you purloined that line. So they've been seeing one another for a while?

Geeze

I'm not sure, and I merely appropriated the line, then changed it slightly, thus making it my own. Never forget the difference between a good writer and a great writer. (Drinking his drink with demonstrable disgust.) If this be liquor, I surely wouldn't kiss her. (Tries another bottle.) A Scotch, a Scotch, my kingdom for a Scotch.

Frieze

Let us away. (Walking back to the group with an inebriated Geeze in tow.)

Louise

So Cheese, who's the best writer you work with?

Cheese

My organization represents a number of talented writers who distinguish themselves in many different ways. A co-worker of mine currently represents a young playwright who may one day cause the world to remember Shakespeare as that fellow who wrote those sonnets.

Louise
(Indicating Wheeze.) How does this one distinguish himself?

Cheese
He has the uncanny knack for not complicating matters. Most writers working today find overly complex answers to simple questions, just breathing becomes an epic for them.

Louise
It sounds like he's got a real gift.

Frieze
(Approaching.) Indeed, he's both a gift recipient and a gift giver. Wheeze always knows precisely what his audience wants, and without exception he obligingly gives it to them. He is a confectioner of the highest order, serving the sweetest treats around. It may not be literature, but it's damn tasty.

Geeze
(In his own world now.) It'll decay your teeth and rot your gut.

Cheese
(To Frieze.) Don't be too proud; hubris comes at a price. I've seen it a dozen times before in other writers, some of whom you know.

Frieze
I have more humility in the tip of my pecker than any of those guys.

Louise

It comes as no surprise to me that you have a humble penis.

Geeze

Humility be hanged. We fictioneers have lost our pioneering mettle. We need to once again find our courage and forge into that undiscovered country. For it was the great white explorer who first found this brave new land of ours.

Frieze

(To Louise.) When he gets racial, it means he's really in the bag.

Wheeze

What about the indigenous peoples?

Geeze

He found them too. It was the great white explorer that first set frozen foot on the North Pole.

Cheese

Actually that was a black fellow.

Geeze

He was probably covered in snow, making him temporarily white. It was the great white explorer that first mounted Mount Everest.

Frieze

And his Sherpa partner.

Geeze

We can't know what went on in that tent of theirs? It was the great white explorer that first pierced the veil of space.

Louise

After they shot all those chimpanzees up there.

Geeze

Chimps trained by pioneers with an unquenchable thirst for
the spirit of exploration.

Frieze

The only spirits your thirst ever compelled you to explore were
eighty proof.

Geeze

I can tell from your spitefully snide remarks that you're against me.

Frieze

I thought my remarks were snidely spiteful. (Geeze begins
leering at Louise.) Maybe we ought to get king leer some coffee.

Cheese

(To Louise as he moves Geeze to the bar.) Forgive him, the
drink too often liberates his tongue, but he'll be back to his
avuncular self again in no time.

Wheeze

We'll let him rest here for a bit. (Cheese helps Wheeze sit Geeze
on a barstool.)

Frieze

Sure, prop him up at the bar where the booze is within arm's reach.

Louise

Maybe you shouldn't encourage your friend to drink so much.

Frieze

It's the alcoholism that does the encouraging.

Louise

Why do you writers imbibe so?

Frieze

I suppose it makes the pain hurt less.

Louise

It's a pity. Legions would give anything to have his talent. Watching him piss it away is as cruel as it is heartbreaking.

Frieze

Are we still talking about Geeze over there?

Louise

I'm talking about all of you sots. My father was a writer...and a drunk.

Frieze

Was he any good?

Louise

As a drunk? Yes. As a writer? Maybe. As a father? No.

Frieze

Try not to be too hard on him. The liquor waters the ideas so they can grow, and then washes them away when they don't bear fruit.

Louise

My father wasn't a drunk when he first started writing, and I doubt Geeze was either. What makes that switch flip?

Frieze

Spending your life creating something from nothing—inventing people who don't exist and situations that never were—makes you feel as if you're always in two places at once, but never completely in either.

Louise

I don't follow. Explain it to me as simply as you can. Don't worry, I'll pretend you used a lot of impressive verbiage.

Frieze

You just feel weird.

Louise

That's it? The whole world is weird.

Frieze

I'm weird. You might be weird. But the whole world can't be weird or weird would be normal. Once I was in line at this deli with seven people in front of me. (The lights dim and the seven actors form a line facing the audience while Frieze narrates.) I'm bored and hungry, and I just want to get my sandwich and go, but standing there, looking at the backs of these seven strangers' heads, I realize I can see inside them. Not their skulls and gray matter, but their motives and ideas. I was seeing their stories. They were the seven ages of man, the seven deadly sins, the seven wonders of the world all right there in that deli. (The line becomes a circle that marches around Frieze, slowly at first and then faster.) At first the sensation was exhilarating, then overwhelming, and then terrifying. I could hear their thoughts like I've never heard anything before. (The actors begin chanting: See me. Hear me. Know me.) The cacophony was so intense that I thought I might vomit. (The actors resume their original positions.)

Louise

(Anxiously.) So what did you do?

Frieze

(Calmly.) I left. But ever since then I slip in and out of that strange, intrusive dimension—whether I want to or not. And if people knew I was doing it, then my weirdness would be that much more confirmed.

Louise

So that'll be you one day too: a drunken, broken-down, has-been writer.

Cheese

(Before Frieze can respond, Cheese returns with Wheeze and they only hear the last part of Louise's statement.) Don't judge him too harshly my dear; he has more than a few demons chasing after him. He just needs to collect himself. He'll be fresh as a daisy once the guests start arriving.

Frieze

If he waits that long, he'll be pushing updaisies.

Cheese

Perhaps people are having a difficult time finding places to park. Did you two have any trouble finding a spot?

Wheeze

We did as a matter of fact. It's really become a problem in this neighborhood—actually all over the city. I still haven't gotten used to it. Back in my hometown there was always plenty of parking; most lots didn't even bother to paint those yellow lines.

Cheese

I'll imagine traffic wasn't an issue either.

Wheeze

There was only one stoplight in town, and it was at the intersection where we had the most accidents.

Frieze

The most hazardous rural intersection is the crossroads where Robert Johnson sold his soul to the devil. (Awkwardly.) I've never had a driver's license, but I wanted to participate in the conversation.

Louise

(Almost to herself.) It seems Geeze was the life of this party.

Wheeze

When people would visit, they always marveled that we never locked our doors, not realizing the futility of a locked door when your nearest neighbor lives a half-mile away.

Frieze

Does a kicked-in door make a sound if there's no one there to hear it?

Wheeze

Quite so. But then it works the other way too. I grew up hearing rumors of prowlers that met their end after waking up a farmer who slept with a shotgun near the bed. No reason to trouble the local sheriff when you own a few hundred acres on which to dig a grave.

Frieze

A shame the Clutter family didn't know that little trick.

Louise

(Quite bored now.) Really, a Truman Capote reference?

Frieze

(Suddenly the lights go out.) On the count of three, let's all try opening our eyes.

Wheeze

I'll check the circuit breaker. I think it's in the backroom.

Frieze

I'll come with you. (The two head for the backroom in the dark.)

Cheese

I shall remain here and protect fair lady.

Louise

Where is the bartender?

Cheese

He doesn't come on until later, or perhaps tomorrow. I really am quite useless when it comes to organizing these events, but I've recently resolved to hire someone to assist me.

Wheeze

(Wheeze and Frieze are attempting to make their way to the backroom. Wheeze calls out to Frieze over his shoulder, thinking Frieze is behind him.) Watch out for the bar.

Frieze

(In front, asking over his shoulder.) What? (Walks into the bar.) Ouch!

Wheeze

Sorry, I thought you were behind me.

Geeze

(From the floor behind the bar.) Who the hell is that?

Frieze

The Ghost of Christmas Past. What are you doing down there old man?

Geeze

Sleeping until you woke me up, you clumsy oaf.

Frieze

Well get up. We need to check the circuit breaker in the back-room.

Geeze

Why?

Frieze

Why? Look around, that's why.

Geeze

I don't see anything.

Frieze

Are you trying to be funny?

                    Geeze

At my age?

                    Wheeze

Geeze, did you turn off the lights?

                    Geeze

Of course I did.

                    Wheeze

And why would you do that?

                    Geeze

This is a surprise party, isn't it? I turned out the lights and hid behind the bar. I must've fallen asleep. Did I miss the surprise?

                    Frieze

You haven't missed anything, but let's get the lights back on.

                    Geeze

Okay. (He stumbles to his feet and fumbles for the light switch. The lights come back on. Geeze is covered in bottle caps and other bar floor detritus.) There, that's better.

                    Louise

You're a mess.

                    Geeze

I am, aren't I? I'll have words with that bartender about sweeping up. Why it's not suitable to take a nap back here.

                    Frieze

Geeze, I've long admired your predilection for old-timey trousers that have a waistline above the naval and a crotch that snuggly cups your man bits.

Geeze

I sense you are about to ask an indelicate question, my boy.

Frieze

Which way do you dress? I only inquire because you have some sort of liquid running down the length of your left pant leg. Is it possible you were lying in a puddle of spilt beer?

Geeze

(Inspecting the stain in question.) Possible yes, though likely no, as it feels warm against my skin.

Cheese

Oh dear. We should run him home.

Wheeze

Louise and I can take him.

Cheese

Nonsense. It's your party. You should stay and receive your guests.

Frieze

Cheese, nobody's coming. We're it.

Cheese

I fear you might be right. Will you help me get him home then?

Frieze

As much as I'd like to, I have someplace else I need to be.

Cheese

At this hour? You young bohemians. (To Wheeze.) Then can I impose upon you for assistance?

Wheeze

Of course, though I see no reason why Louise should have to share in this unpleasant task.

Cheese

Nor do I. We can take my car.

Wheeze

(Handing Louise his car keys.) I'll meet you later.

Louise

Sure.

Cheese

(To Frieze.) Will you be able to secure your own transportation?

Louise

Oh, I can drop him.

Cheese

Most kind of you. We should be getting this one home to bed. (Cheese and Wheeze each take hold of Geeze and escort him to the door.)

Geeze

(Mumbling to Frieze as he leaves.) Fire in water will save you.

Frieze

Firewater will save me? Remind me to never ask you for advice.

Geeze

(Crossly.) No, fire in water— (The three exit.)

Louise

Do you know what he was saying?

Frieze

I haven't a clue what he was prattling on about.

Louise

Fire in water—he meant…here. (She puts her hand on his chest and the tension between them builds.) Where can I take you?

Frieze

Are you and Wheeze—

Louise

No…not really.

Frieze

Then take me to your place or mine if you prefer. I have a piano.

Louise

Why don't we just go for a walk? (Frieze turns off the lights and they exit together.)

Epilogue

(Back in prison. Everyone but the Steward stands behind Frieze, though he does not see them.)

Frieze

Steward, are you still there?

Steward

Yes.

Frieze

Working here must have availed you of some insight into death. What's it like when you die?

Steward

You know that light at the end of the tunnel people talk about?

Frieze

Sure.

Steward

They really see it. But I don't think it's the entrance to any afterlife. I think that bright light is nature's way of getting you to shut your eyelids before you kick, so the living don't have to look into the eyes of the dead.

Frieze

That's some cold comfort. (To himself now.) I never did one brave thing in my whole life. If I had another life to live I'd probably just waste that one too. (He removes the cover from the dish and smells the food.)Louise.

Steward

What?

Frieze

The name of my first love.

Steward

Oh.

Frieze

But it did take me a moment. (Breaks the fortune cookie and eats it.)

What Does a Question Weigh?

A Play
by

WES PAYTON

Characters

Lieutenant —a hard-boiled detective with the Chicago police department who doubts the veracity of Tralf's claims

Tralf —a self-described alien anthropologist who says he has traveled to our time to discover a cure for the lethal ennui of his time

McGuffin —a Chicago luminary whose wife has gone missing

Sergeant —a female police officer

Captain —boss to the Lieutenant and Sergeant

Blographer —Tralf's blogger-biographer

Bomber —a young anarchist (can be played by Young FBI Agent)

Old FBI Agent —senior FBI agent

Young FBI Agent —rookie FBI agent, non-native speaker

The action occurs on a bifurcated stage.

ACT ONE

Scene I

(The Sergeant and the Blographer wait quietly in the interrogation room on the left side of the stage.)

Sergeant

So you just follow Tralf around and write stories about him on the Internet?

Blographer

I'm his blographer…so essentially, yes.

Sergeant

(After a long pause.) Is he really from the future?

Captain

(Entering.) Sergeant, who is this person?

Sergeant

He's a writer, Captain.

Captain

I had understood that this matter hadn't leaked to the press yet.

Blographer

I'm not a reporter. I'm Mister Tralf's blographer, and I can delay my next post until the story breaks, if you like.

Captain

McGuffin said he was bringing counsel with him, which I just learned two minutes ago isn't his attorney but rather this time-traveling busybody, and now I'm expected to allow press to attend his deposition?

Blographer

Mister Tralf and I are a package deal.

Captain

And what if I say you aren't?

Blographer

Then I go home and write what I have now. My readership is larger than the population of our Windy City. It'll give the country something to talk about over morning coffee.

Captain

Are you trying to blackmail me?

Blographer

More like strong-arm, but then you're the boss; we can call it whatever you want.

Captain

I miss the days when the police were in charge.

Sergeant

(After a pause.) So Captain, you think Tralf is from the future, too?

Captain

Absolutely not. He's a grifter who preys on the gullible—a charlatan. The script may change but not the hustle.

Sergeant

(Another pause.) So how far in the future is he from?

Blographer

Ten generations.

Sergeant

So about a hundred and fifty years—that doesn't seem like so long.

Captain

It'd be twice that much.

Sergeant

How do you figure, Captain?

Captain

A generation is every thirty years or so.

Sergeant

I'm not sure about that. I mean we're three generations right here: I'm young, he's middle-aged, and you're old—generationally speaking, sir.

Captain

It doesn't work that way. I'm middle-aged because I'm only old enough to be your father—not your grandfather. So there are only two generations here.

Sergeant

Then which generation is he? (Indicating Blographer.)

Captain

Definitely yours.

Sergeant

Begging your pardon, but he's not in my generation.

Captain

Let's count off the generations from the last century. The Lost Generation was World War I; the Greatest Generation was World War II; the Baby Boomers were Vietnam; and Generation X was Iraq. Each generation has its war.

Sergeant

See that doesn't work because my dad served in Iraq the first time when I was in grade school, and I did two tours over there this last time.

Blographer

Here they come.
(Tralf and McGuffin enter the interrogation room followed by the Lieutenant. Tralf paces as McGuffin sits at the table. The Lieutenant briefly confers with the Sergeant and Captain. The Blographer moves to the far corner.)

Lieutenant

So tell me again why he's here. (Pointing to Tralf.)

McGuffin

As I explained, he is my counsel.

Lieutenant

That explanation made more sense when I thought that meant he was an attorney.

Captain

Furthermore Mr. McGuffin, we have no intention of charging you with anything. After all, you came to us about your wife's disappearance.

McGuffin

Abduction.

Captain

Of course, my point though is that in our eyes you're above suspicion in this matter, considering that there would be no matter for us to investigate had you not brought it to our attention, so therefore you need no counsel. We only wish to gather what details we can from you so that we can begin our investigation.

McGuffin

Tralf is not here as my legal counsel but rather to assist with your investigatory efforts. You'll find him quite resourceful.

Lieutenant

You must be joking. We ain't gonna let this lunatic go mucking up our investigation, provided that your wife really has been abducted and hasn't just gone off on some shopping spree without telling you.

Captain

What my passionate but capable Lieutenant is trying to say is that there are many possible explanations for your wife's disappearance and that our efforts to get to the bottom of this matter would only be hindered by outside interference.

McGuffin

Captain, it is not that I doubt your sincerity, it's that I doubt your ability. Tralf is already on the job. He had begun to investigate my wife's abduction the moment we became aware that she was missing. He has access to all my properties and an intimate knowledge of my family's history—even the hush-hush bits—not to mention his keen powers of reasoning and deduction.

Sergeant

You just did mention it—twice.

Lieutenant

He sounds like a prime suspect to me.

Captain

Yes, I must agree with the sentiments, if not the tone, of my subordinates. This is most irregular.

McGuffin

If you think he's a suspect then interview him if you wish. You will find him the acme of accommodating, though it is becoming clear to me that the reverse will not be so. Nevertheless, Tralf will be investigating this matter—either in concert with your department or independent of it. (Letting the point sink in for a moment.) Well, I must be off. Let me know when you know something.

Captain

We will indeed. We'll assign the Sergeant here as your liaison. We'll need someone from our department with you at all times for when the kidnappers contact you with their ransom demands.

McGuffin

Of course, though I'll be in Tokyo next week for the G7 summit.

Captain

Right, is there any way we can convince you to cancel your trip?

McGuffin

The President would be quite cross. She's sponsoring the presentation I'm giving on the viability of my Prairie-Grassoline initiative.

Captain

Ever been to Japan, Sergeant?

Sergeant

No, Captain.

Lieutenant

You take in any sights and we're docking your vacation leave.

Sergeant

Yes, Lieutenant.

Captain

Sergeant, drive Mr. McGuffin home.

McGuffin

Nonsense, my driver is here, and besides it wouldn't do to have me seen in one of your squad cars.

Sergeant

I drive an unmarked.

McGuffin

Yes, well your presence would have a way of marking it, I suspect. I shall leave word with the doorman to expect you. Best of luck. (Exits.)

(The Sergeant, Lieutenant, and Captain move to the observation room on the right side of the stage.)

Sergeant

Wow, that guy's an asshole.

Lieutenant

I guess he can afford to be.

Captain

Why do I feel like we all work for him now?

Lieutenant

What he pays in property taxes is as much as we'd get from our combined pensions if we each lived to be a hundred.

Sergeant

So you like him for the kidnapping, right?

Lieutenant

Of course. He pays some foreign goons to snatch his wife. A day from now they'll send a proof of life with a ransom note. The drop will go south. In a week we'll find her shot through the head in a dumpster. In a month's time we'll nab some guy that never heard the name McGuffin trying to pawn the deceased wife's jewelry. He'll fry and our environmentally clean suspect will be wife-less, alimony-less, and untouchable.

Sergeant

Ever the pessimist.

Lieutenant

If I was an optimist, I wouldn't be any good at my job.

Captain

So how do we make sure all that doesn't happen?

Lieutenant

Let's interrogate shit-for-brains in there. Obviously he's here to throw us off the scent, but maybe we can turn that against him.

Captain

Sure, but don't underestimate him. I pulled his file. He took the police officers' exam a couple years back and aced the cognitive assessment portion. Never been done by anyone before, present company included.

Sergeant

So how come he's still a civilian?

Lieutenant

He thinks he's from another planet. How could he pass the Psych?

Sergeant

He's not from another planet. He's from this planet...just from the future.

Lieutenant

Let's talk to his biographer first. (Opens the door to the interrogation room.) You, come here.

Biographer

Me?

Lieutenant

Hurry up.

Biographer

(Entering.) I really shouldn't be involved. Think of me as a fly on the wall.

Lieutenant

Okay, if you don't answer our questions we'll swat ya, and we SWAT hard.

Captain

We only want a little background information on your friend in there. What can you tell us that might be useful?

Biographer

Useful for what?

Lieutenant

We'll ask the questions.

Biographer

Listen Officer Cliché, this Bad Lieutenant routine won't work on me, I know—

Lieutenant

Sergeant, you dropped your pen. Let me be a gentleman and pick it up for you. (The Sergeant tosses her pen on the floor between the Blographer's legs. The Lieutenant quickly bends over and jabs the Blographer in the crotch as he retrieves the pen. The Blographer winces in pain.) Watch it there, this pen almost poked you in the nuts. That would've been embarrassing.

Captain

I imagine you live in a pricey condo in a nice part of town. You make good money doing this, don't you? All we're asking is that you earn your keep.

Blographer

(Trying to shake off the injury.) What do you want to know?

Lieutenant

What the hell kind of name is Tralf, anyway?

Captain

According to our records, he was born Trey Alfonse.

Blographer

He started calling himself Tralf when he became aware that he was from the future.

Sergeant

I thought that he was born in the future.

Blographer

He was. He volunteered for a time-traveling project in his time when he was thirty. His mind was digitized and sent ten generations back through his family bloodline, where the genetic payload was implanted at the moment of Trey's conception. When his ancestor reached the age that Tralf was when he left his own time—

Sergeant

He became Tralf; he became aware of himself.

Lieutenant

I'm glad you're following this.

Captain

That's all very interesting, but not the least bit helpful. Give us something else.

Blographer

Okay, his mind…the human brain of his time is significantly more evolved than ours.

Lieutenant

So, what's that mean?

Blographer

That means you should think of his mind as an exotic sports car, capable of tremendous speed and precision, but also far more delicate than the pickup trucks we drive. He's a man with no subconscious. He is always thinking about something. His mind is never empty, never at rest. If he stopped thinking, even for a moment, his mind would shut down and he'd die, like a shark that stopped swimming. When he sleeps, he falls instantly into an REM state and his dreams are inexorably logical—not irrational like ours.

Captain

That's preposterous. How could you possibly know what he dreams about?

Lieutenant

Besides, everyone is always thinking. When someone asks what we're thinking about and we say "nothing," that just means we're thinking about something we shouldn't.

Blographer

Maybe, but believe me his mind is not like ours. Cop tricks won't work on him, though you won't need to use any. He never lies.

Lieutenant

If he told you that then it proves he's a liar.

Blographer

No, he's incapable of lying. He simply doesn't understand how.

Lieutenant

You just say something that isn't true—that's how.

Blographer

Things that may seem simple to us can be complicated for him, and things that are complicated for us are simple to him.

Lieutenant

The world often seems simple to the simple-minded.

Captain

We can do without all this double-talk. Give us more.

Blographer

What's another…oh, the way they see—their vision.

Lieutenant

What are you gonna tell us now—that they see with their hands and fart out their ears?

Blographer

No, their vision is based on movement, so they can devote their full mental capacity to, well, more important matters rather than the ocular processing that engages much of our hippocampus. That's why Tralf doesn't appreciate static art, such as sculpture or photography—

Sergeant

Because there's no movement.

Blographer

Precisely.

Captain

What else?

Blographer

Well, their math is on a base-twelve system; I haven't figured out why yet.

Sergeant

Why not just ask him?

Blographer

He's here to study our culture—not to explain his.

Lieutenant

Base twelve-system—I think that's plenty. Let's go talk to David Bowie in there. Maybe he can tell me who's gonna win the World Series. (To Blographer.) You stay here. (The Lieutenant, Sergeant, and Captain enter the interrogation room.)

Sergeant

(To the Captain.) Who's David Bowie?

Captain

A musician his generation listens to.

Lieutenant

All right shit stain, we're on to you. You might be able to fool some folks with too much money and too little sense, but we work for a living; we know the score. Here's how I see it. Your boss throws you in with us, to get us off the trail back to him. The way I figure, he paid some guys to nab his wife and then off her, if they haven't already. Makes sense to me—cheaper than a divorce and maybe he parlays some of that widower sympathy into a bid for public office. He's using you as a blocking dummy on his run to the White House. See you've got it twisted; you think you're bilking him, but he's really scamming you. (Pause.) Aren't you going to say something? What's Tralf short for anyway—trifling asshole?

Tralf

What is Lieutenant long for—lie?

Lieutenant

Is that supposed to be funny?

Tralf

I hope so. We do not have humor in my time, so I am not very adept at invoking it, and I was not certain if "Lieutenant" was still spelled in old way in your time. If I may ask, what are your names?

Lieutenant

Sure you may ask. This here is Sergeant Fuck-you, that's our boss Captain Fuck-you, and me I'm Lieutenant Fuck-you.

Tralf

So you are all related. That is nice. Butcher, baker, and candlestick maker.

Lieutenant

How's that?

Tralf

That is what I will call you. Sergeant Butcher, Lieutenant Baker, and Captain Candlestick.

Lieutenant

What's that make you then?

Tralf

I suppose vegetarian on no-carb diet who uses electricity for light.

Lieutenant

Meaning?

Tralf

I want to help you, but I do not need your help.

Lieutenant

I have a real short attention span for stupidity, so you can skip all the alien archeologist tom-fuckery.

Tralf

Archeologists dig.

Lieutenant

You messing with me?

Tralf

No, merely correcting you. It would be more accurate to say that I am alien anthropologist, though alien in sense that I come from another time—not another place.

Lieutenant

That's the thing with crazy people, they don't know they're crazy. So they spell "Lieutenant" different in your time?

Tralf

We do not use word "Lieutenant." My time has no ranks. However, when global language accord was enacted several generations ago spellings of many words were abbreviated.

Lieutenant

So the whole world speaks English in the future?

Tralf

Hybrid form of English known as Unbabel.

Lieutenant

So the Chinese and the Mexicans, they speak English?

Tralf

My time has no countries.

Lieutenant

(In a singsong voice.) I bet your time ain't got no religion too.

Tralf

Correct.

Lieutenant

All right then heathen, how many apostles did Jesus have?

Tralf

After or before Judas hanged himself?

Lieutenant

How many months in a year—in my time?

Tralf

One dozen.

Lieutenant

Hours in a day?

Tralf

Two dozen.

Lieutenant

Seconds in a minute.

Tralf

Five dozen.

Lieutenant

You like baseball?

Tralf

Very much.

Lieutenant

How many innings in a non-rain-out game when the home team doesn't bat last?

Tralf

Three-quarters dozen.

Lieutenant

Where's Mrs. McGuffin?

Tralf

At the bottom of Lake Michigan. (The Sergeant and Captain move closer to Tralf.)

Lieutenant

Say that again?

Tralf

Four days ago Mr. and Mrs. McGuffin left for lake cruise on their sailing yacht. According to Mr. McGuffin they returned late last night. Mr. McGuffin says he fell asleep on divan in sitting room and discovered Mrs. McGuffin's abduction this morning when he awoke. Doorman was not on duty at time when Mr. McGuffin says they arrived at their building and their garage security camera was in process of being repaired. I believe Mrs. McGuffin never returned. I believe Mr. McGuffin cast his wife overboard into lake.

Lieutenant

Is that so? Well, I believe that you're full of shit.

Tralf

No, what you believe is that I am here to sabotage your investigation, but opposite is true. Without witnesses you have very little chance of proving Mr. McGuffin's guilt. Without me you have almost none.

Lieutenant

Then tell me, why would McGuffin offer your help if you're the only one who can prove he's guilty.

Tralf

I doubt I can prove his guilt, but I am nearly certain that you cannot. As for why Mr. McGuffin insisted on my presence, reasons are threefold. As you said before, I am prime suspect, especially once you discover nature of relationship I had with Mrs. McGuffin. Secondly, Mrs. McGuffin was my good friend and Mr. McGuffin is villain through and through, so he enjoys how my involvement tortures me. Finally, it makes game more interesting for him.

Lieutenant

You think I'm playing games?

Tralf

No, and neither am I. However, I can assure you that Mr. McGuffin is.

Sergeant

Why don't we just search the lake?

Captain

You could sink Vermont and New Hampshire in those waters and still have room leftover for Delaware.

Sergeant

Well, she'd have to float ashore eventually.

Lieutenant

Like the man said, it's a big lake.

Sergeant

But the ship must have a GPS log; we could retrace his route.

Tralf

Mr. McGuffin eschews modern technology on his vintage boats.

Captain

Besides, if she's been in open water for even a few hours, her body could've drifted almost anywhere.

Sergeant

What's the name of his ship?

Tralf

Hunter. It is Dutch translation of word "yacht."

Lieutenant

And how do you spell "yacht" in Unbabel?

Tralf

Y-O-T. We use our vowels differently.

Lieutenant

You know you still don't add up for me. What's your stake in all this? You say you and the late Mrs. McGuffin had a thing, if she is in fact no longer with us—God forbid. The way I understand it, Mr. McGuffin doesn't exactly spend a lot of his nights at home. I hear he's got birds cooped up all over town. So what's he care about you and her?

Tralf

She was like prized ornament for him—shiny thing to be displayed. Our relationship tarnished that perception.

Lieutenant

Okay then. But why boot her off his boat into the lake? McGuffin strikes me as a planner. Why not something more foolproof, like she dies on a ski trip in the Alps while he's installing solar panels or some shit in Africa? Or even this whole kidnapping gone south scenario?

Tralf

It would not be compelling game for him if there were no risk. McGuffin enjoys being study of contrasts, both savior and sinner. He believes that is only way to make most of human experience. He is child testing his boundaries, wanting to know what he can get away with, and you people bestowed unlimited resources upon him. I doubt he intended to do her harm when they sailed out of Belmont Harbor. Likely it was sudden thought that flashed in his head as sun slipped behind cloud and he knew that his pernicious act would go unseen.

Lieutenant

Maybe, but how can you be sure?

Tralf

Way he looked at her had grown darker in recent weeks. It is look that is common in my time.

Lieutenant

You got a lot of murdering jealous husbands where you come from?

Tralf

When I come from there is only one crime, and it has no punishment save consequence resulting from crime itself.

Lieutenant

That must make the cops happy.

Tralf

My time has no police.

Sergeant

What's the one crime?

Tralf

Self-murder.

Sergeant

Why would anyone want to kill themselves in your era? From what I've read your time is a utopia—no poverty, no disease.

Lieutenant

Let's let the future worry about the future, while we focus on the here and now.

Tralf

I concur.

Captain

Tralf, I know you're smart, but how is it that you speak our English so well, aside from dropping your "a"s and "the"s?

Lieutenant

Captain, please. This is a possible homicide investigation?

Captain

If he's to help us, we'd do well to understand him.

Tralf

Training in my time for this operation was substantial. Also, I can access most of memories and education of my ancestor before I replaced him. As for articles, my time does not use them, and neglecting to use them now is bad habit I have heretofore been unable to break.

Captain

That puzzles me too. You say you've taken over your ancestor's life, but won't that alter the future?

Tralf

My ancestor's only documented contribution was fathering child at age twenty-six, whom he promptly abandoned. Records suggest that he spent remainder of his life as drifter. That is one reason why I was viable candidate.

Sergeant

What if he made some unaccounted for contribution?

Captain

Or perhaps you will make some sort of contribution, thus altering your past and our future.

Tralf

I fear I already have. According to our records Mrs. McGuffin lived to age eighty-three.

Lieutenant

Wait, you studied her before you came here to our time? Fuck me, now I'm getting caught up in this too.

Tralf

Mrs. McGuffin was identified as a potential patron who would be sympathetic to my cause. She introduced me to publisher who—

Sergeant

Your book of poetry—*Dozavo*. I read it when I was stationed overseas. It really spoke to me—all that stuff about feeling like an outsider in strange and violent times. What were those poems called?

Tralf

Dodec-ikus. It was my publisher's idea to call them that.

Lieutenant

Hold on, just when this starts to make a little sense it gets even more ridiculous. You're telling me that you're a fucking poet, like Jack Frost or somebody?

Tralf

Robert Frost. Not at all. The book was merely journal of my logs that I had reported back to my time.

Sergeant

Each poem—I mean log—is twelve lines long, with the first line having twelve syllables on down to the last line, which just has one.

Tralf

That is only way transmissions can be deciphered in my time.

Lieutenant

You're still in contact with your time?

Tralf

I make report twice daily, at noon and midnight.

Lieutenant

I can't believe I'm even going to ask this, but why the hell don't you just find out what happened to Mrs. McGuffin from your friends in the future?

Tralf

My reports can only travel with flow of time into future. No communication can be sent against flow.

Lieutenant

Except you were sent back against the flow?

Tralf

I was transmitted through gene legacy sequence—different rules apply.

Lieutenant

How *con*-venient.

Tralf

Think of it as difference between sending email and shouting at someone from across street. Neither text of email or sound of voice has weight. After all, information has no intrinsic mass—only its medium can. Whether etched in stone or written in sand, Dozen Minus Couple Commandments have same meaning. Both your emails and your voice can be sent through time, but whereas identical email can be forwarded again and again through Internet system, words you shout cannot be forwarded; they exist exactly way you first shouted them only once. You can repeat words, but they would not be precisely same sounds. Perhaps your voice strains second time or traffic changes. It is same with my reports; they exist only once. I shout them into future and they are retrieved in my time. Conversely, I came to be here now as series of reversed forwards through dozen minus couple generations of my ancestry system.

Lieutenant

That all just sounds like bullshit.

Tralf

I grant you it is not something that Newtonians can easily grasp.

Sergeant

So then how will you return to your time?

Tralf

I cannot. I will die here in this time, in this body.

Captain

And your ancestor will never have his life back?

Tralf

(Irritation that crescendos to anger.) I am not here on holiday. I am here for information that might save my people. We are self-murdering at twice birth rate. In three generations human race will be all but extinct. Do you understand? My ancestor's sacrifice in this time is insignificant compared to all-murder of my time!

Lieutenant

Okay, don't get bent out of shape, future-boy.

Tralf

I apologize. I sometimes have difficulty controlling my impulses in this vessel.

Lieutenant

Sure, just take a minute to pull yourself together, and we'll be right back.

Lieutenant

(Exiting to the observation room with the Sergeant and Captain.) You should go check on your meal ticket.

Blographer

What did you do to him? (Enters the interrogation room in a panic.)

Lieutenant

Okay, I'll admit it. He's way more of a nut-job than I first gave him credit for.

Captain

But you can't deny his intelligence, and I've encountered enough pretend crazies to know that he genuinely believes what he's telling us.

Sergeant

You two still don't think he's legit?

Captain

Legitimately from the future? Of course not. Legitimately insane? To be sure. But that doesn't mean he wouldn't be an asset to this investigation.

Lieutenant

I don't like what I think you're going to say next.

Captain

McGuffin's agreed to give us access if Tralf's attached to this inquiry. Maybe if McGuffin thinks we're buying into his game, he'll let down his guard and slip up.

Lieutenant

How can you be of the opinion that he's a wacko and that we should accept his help? Christ, let's just go ahead and deputize him? Hell, we'll save some paper and write up his department contract on the back of my letter of resignation. We can even recycle my badge to him. That should please his eco-highness, Lord McGuffin!

Captain

Are you quite finished Lieutenant? I have no intention of deputizing anyone or accepting anyone's resignation. I simply believe it might be helpful to have him tag along for the initial stages of this investigation. Maybe Tralf will unknowingly reveal something. Or maybe not. But unless you think the better alternative is to have the entire U.S. Coast Guard start dragging Lake Michigan, let's play it this way for now.

Lieutenant

Fine Captain. Because I don't think any of this is the least bit ri-cock-ulous, I say fine.

Captain

Since I detect no sarcasm in your voice, I'll consider the matter settled. Sergeant, take a detail over to McGuffin's building. Post officers at all the P-O-Es. You stay with McGuffin.

Lieutenant

You keep on him at all times. If he takes a shit, I want you there holding the toilet paper.

Captain

I'll notify the forensics team and have them meet you there.

Lieutenant

Tell the CSIs to run some testicles for anomalous, latent prints—both kinds, foot and finger.

Sergeant

What's that going to turn up?

Lieutenant

Probably nothing, but it'd be useful to know that too. And keep your team out of the rich man's liquor cabinet.

Sergeant

It's great having two bosses. Radio if you need anything. (Exits.)

Captain

What is it with sarcasm and your generation?

Lieutenant

She's not part of my generation.

Captain

Well, you and your new partner better get at it. (Exits.)

Lieutenant

(Entering the interrogation room.) Come along then Deputy Fuck-you. We're going on a stakeout—undercover and such. You ever been on a stakeout?

Tralf

I have spent whole of my sojourn in this time on stakeout, so to speak.

Lieutenant

Uh huh. (To Blographer who rises to leave with them.) Uh uh, not you William Shit-speare. Just 'cause you're his shower partner don't make you his cop partner.

Tralf

We are not shower partners…though I suppose you were just being disdainful. (To Blographer.) In this situation I believe two can observe better than three, so it is with regret that I say you may not join us; however, I genuinely doubt you will miss anything of interest.

Blographer

I understand.

Tralf

Also, please have invitations for upcoming Doubleday event sent to Sergeant, Lieutenant, and Captain.

Scene II

(On stakeout sitting in a parked car in front of an apartment building. The Bomber tinkers with a device at a work table on the dark half of the stage.)

Lieutenant

The tech boys have been monitoring recent Internet chatter concerning some nasty shenanigans targeted at a few of our city's green industry big wigs. Your boss ain't been mentioned by name yet, but it's the only lead we got. They triangulated the IP address to this apartment building, but they ain't got any idea which unit it's coming from. So just keep your eyes open for suspicious types—not including yourself that is.

Tralf

I am not employed by Mr. McGuffin. I would never work for someone I despise.

Lieutenant

You keep sayin' that, and I keep not believin' you.

Tralf

What one believes and what one knows to be fact often inhabit two distinct realities.

Lieutenant

You're a trip all right. There anymore like you where you come from?

Tralf

There was another traveler to this time. Her name was Anthrope. I met her once before she self- murdered. Self-murder is tantamount to failure in this mission.

Lieutenant

No I meant—(the Lieutenant's mobile phone rings)—hang on. (He answers it.) Yeah. Uh huh. Okay...okay I'll talk to her later. (Pause.) Right, her recital fundraiser thing. Yeah, I know the drill. My job is to clap and spend money. I'll keep my opinions to myself. (Pause.) She said what? Uh huh...uh huh. (Pause.) Holy shit, something huge just happened here—big crisis— gotta go! (Ending the phone call.) That was my girlfriend. Seems my daughter called her a bitch. Or actually a "bumble bee itch." Cute, ain't it?

Tralf

She likely learned to use vulgar language by example.

Lieutenant

Probably, those little shits at her school can be real foul mouths. I'll bet she hears words on the playground that could expand a sailor's vocabulary. What would you know about it anyway? You ain't got any kids, do you—at least that you had since after you became you?

Tralf

No, nor can I ever have offspring. When I became myself again, I underwent vasectomy to eliminate possibility of disrupting my ancestry system.

Lieutenant

You really do shop at Crazy-mart.

Tralf

What will you do about your daughter's behavior?

Lieutenant

Christ I don't know, maybe give her a raise in allowance.

Tralf

You blaspheme great deal.

Lieutenant

At least I believe.

Tralf

Are conversations between you and your girlfriend always so strained?

Lieutenant

How the hell do you know they're strained?

Tralf

I have developed sense for such matters.

Lieutenant

Is that some sort of aptitude that people from the future have?

Tralf

Not more so than in this time, as far as I have observed.

Lieutenant

I guess she's been puttin' a little pressure on me lately about her upcoming birthday. I can't figure out what to get her. I messed up good and plenty last year when I gave her a Taser.

Tralf

Thoughtful, in its way.

Lieutenant

She didn't think it was romantic. But then when I got her a naughty Mrs. Claus outfit for Christmas, she didn't like that either. There's no pleasing this woman.

Tralf

Give her something you two can participate in together...perhaps sports related, like golf clubs or tennis racquet.

Lieutenant

I got her a set of golf clubs the Christmas before last, but I couldn't teach her nothin'. She's as dumb as a stump when it comes to sports.

Tralf

Perhaps blame lies with instructor. Why not give her some lessons with professional?

Lieutenant

Nah, all that stuff those greasy pros pull with their arms wrapped around a lady's waist...get a firm grip on the shaft, position the head just so, keep your eye on the ball—forget it.

(Time passes.)

Lieutenant

So what did you do in your time, for work I mean?

Tralf

I will be counter.

Lieutenant

Is that your way of saying you were an accountant?

Tralf

My time has no money, so we have no accountants.

Lieutenant

You really just counted stuff, huh? Sounds dull.

Tralf

Quite opposite actually. It is considered rather prestigious vocation. I will have lowest incidence of error at my firm.

Lieutenant

You have to go to school for something like that?

Tralf

I will earn advanced degrees in numeric tallying.

Lieutenant

So what sorts of things do you count?

Tralf

Most high-profile assignment I will have is counting strands of hair of one of my time's preeminent performers, after she commits self-murder. It took me half-dozen days to ensure I had count right.

Lieutenant

Lot of time to spend with a dead person. Why not just make up a number? Or go with the first count and be done with it?

Tralf

Because I will be good at what I do. After all, you do not just make up evidence or arrest first suspect and be done with it.

Lieutenant

Not usually no, but that's different. I mean who the hell cares about her exact number of hair follicles?

Tralf

She will be considered great beauty—last redhead. Perhaps someone from your time should not question my time's obsession with celebrity.

Lieutenant

I've gotta say, most people are boring and full of shit—at least you're not boring. (Pause.) So why leave such a cush job to come to this godless time.

Tralf

For same reason I will become counter I suppose. I wanted answers to questions.

Lieutenant

What questions?

Tralf

Film media of this generation has always fascinated me. Why does your time make so many motion pictures and television programs with themes of law and justice? Why so much interest in criminal minds, such fascination for those who inflict misery?

Lieutenant

You don't have cop shows in your time? Let me guess, your time has no TVs.

Tralf

We do in manner of speaking, but new film programs will no longer be produced. We will watch what people in past watched—what you watch. Our libraries contain lifetimes of your programs.

Lieutenant

Is that how you studied us? Is that why you wanted to be a cop, because of TV and the movies?

Tralf

These shows led me to believe that if I were detective no mystery would ever be unsolvable, no answer too elusive. (Pause.) You are talented interrogator. What techniques do you find most effective for getting information?

Lieutenant

Well, let's see…if you can, always ask two questions at once. Never ask a question that has a "yes" or "no" answer. And try not to ask too many questions that you don't already know the answers to, all while trying to sound uniformed and not particularly interested in the answers.

(More time passes.)

Lieutenant

So your vision's not really based on movement then?

Tralf

Of course not. How would I read?

Lieutenant

You could shake the book.

Tralf

I suppose so. Why would you believe such absurd notion?

Lieutenant

I didn't believe it exactly, it just kind of made sense—what with you not liking static art.

Tralf

What is static art? How do you mean that?

Lieutenant

You know, art that doesn't move, like paintings.

Tralf

I see. I thought you meant something else. Your language is so imprecise.

Lieutenant

You mean my personal language or language at large?

Tralf

All art in my time is considered static. There has been no progress or significant developments in any artistic medium for generations—just reiterations and repetition. Occasionally provocateur will claim original idea, but when piece is unveiled it is inevitably offensive disappointment. Art appreciation is not cultivated in my time's culture. (Pause.) Why do you not execute murderers in your time?

Lieutenant

Where the hell did that come from? Weren't we just having a nice conversation about art and language and what not?

Tralf

I thought that conversation had come to conclusion. I was beginning another.

Lieutenant

It was quite a change of gears…caught me by surprise is all. Do they have executions in your time—that don't seem too civilized? Wait, that's right…you ain't got murderers in your time.

Tralf

Correct, but only because their kind was done away with long ago. Measure was perceived as purging cancerous element to facilitate healthy society.

Lieutenant

Didn't the ACL or somebody make a fuss?

Tralf

ACLU. Your time's priorities will not be my time's priorities. People will realize there are far too many who can benefit from compassion to waste it on those who do not deserve it. You insult good when you put evil first. Such aberrant persons ought to be removed from gene pool. It is not punishment, it is Darwinist imperative. In two generations you would have solved murder problem. Your squeamishness is disservice to your grandchildren

Lieutenant

It could always be better and it could always be worse, and that will only be a lie twice in your whole lifetime. When I was young I was reckless on the job and didn't care if I lived or died. Now I've got an ex-wife I can't get over, a daughter who can't stand me, a girlfriend I can't stand, a drinking problem I can't kick, crippling debt I can't pay, and diverticulitis to boot. And I hope to live to be a hundred and forty-four.

Tralf

A dozen dozen. You have become person of great interest to me.

(More time passes.)

Lieutenant

So why were you chosen? Why did your people pick you for this assignment?

Tralf

There will be many reasons.

Lieutenant

The short answer.

Tralf

I am perspicacious and perspicuous.

Lieutenant

Okay, I'll pretend I know what that means. Why can't you just do all this research from your own time. Why go to the hassle of coming here?

Tralf

Our research of your time will yield nothing that would ameliorate issues in my time.

Lieutenant

You mean suicide? People have been killing themselves since there've been people. It's a uniquely human act. But life is peaks and valleys—maybe your people will come out of their rut.

Tralf

As compelling as your theory is, I do not think it is wise to test it with fate of human race in balance.

Lieutenant

People off themselves these days because of shame and disappointment. Why do they do it in your time?

Tralf

I am not sure...ennui perhaps. There have been extensive studies of course, but findings have been inconclusive. It is said that mind of self-murderer spontaneously chooses to destroy itself. In my time we are inoculated against all physiological eventualities that result in premature death, and some have theorized that minds revolt against unnatural state by corrupting itself rather than body it inhabits.

Lieutenant

And that's when they get that look in their eyes.

Tralf

There is no reaching them at that point. It is only matter of time.

Lieutenant

So what's your take on it?

Tralf

I am not mind scientist.

Lieutenant

You must have some idea.

Tralf

Motion picture *Singing in Rain* is favorite in my time and of mine personally as well. Umbrella typifies backward thinking of this time. Rather than seeking to control precipitation, you instead choose to wield devices to deal with rain.

Lieutenant

That's why you like the movie, so you can mock our simple ways and look down at us as Grace Kelly dances around in puddles.

Tralf

Gene Kelly. That is reason why my people enjoy it; my reasons are somewhat different. I appreciate your time's capacity for finding joy in trying circumstances. In my time we will have conquered weather, solved mysteries of science, and tamed volatilities of economics. We will end all human suffering but never ask if that suffering has purpose. So many aspects of my time will be manipulated and improved that when we encounter something we cannot control, such as self-murder of loved one, our psyches fracture a little. Eventually those fractures become fissures from which there is no escape. Your time resolves to cope whereas my time resolves to change. That has been our success and that will be our demise.

Lieutenant

Well, you ain't gonna find the answer to that mystery through interrogation.

Tralf

I believe answer might be found in your tacit systems.

Lieutenant

I'll probably regret asking, but what's a tacit system?

Tralf

Innate understanding of how human created system works and is therefore never explicitly explained in media. What is axiomatic in your time is enigmatic in mine.

Lieutenant

An example?

Tralf

Fashion and religion—both fluid, perception-based systems and both quite mystery to us.

Lieutenant

Those two hardly seem comparable.

Tralf

Both involve ever-changing trends that obey strict tenets, which are each rife with contradictions.

Lieutenant

What contradictions?

Tralf

Offering inclusion while fostering exclusion.

Lieutenant

Churches feed the hungry and house the homeless.

Tralf

Much philanthropy occurs under aegis of fashion industry.

Lieutenant

Just because some people who look like razorblades parade down a catwalk wearing ridiculous costumes to raise a few bucks for other people who look like razorblades that can't afford the clothes made in the sweatshops their kids work at, don't make Hugo Boss the Pope.

(The Bomber receives a telephone call, answers, listens, hangs up, puts the device in a backpack, and exits off dark side of stage.)

Lieutenant

(Quite bored now. Tallying the people that walk past.) Duck. Duck. Duck.

Tralf

(Also bored, thinking out loud.) Why would goose give chase? Expression is "wild goose chase," not "wild goose chaser." It would make more sense if tapper was goose.

Lieutenant

Duck. Duck. Duck.

Tralf

Plural form should be gooses. Post-middle English is so unnecessarily complicated. Why must another word for multiple gooses be learned when simply adding "s" at end of singular form would suffice as it does for most other nouns?

Lieutenant

Duck. Duck. Duck.

Tralf

Do you think goose that laid golden egg was disappointed?

Lieutenant

Duck. Duck. Duck.

Tralf

(Noticing the Bomber.) That person leaving building with backpack seems somewhat suspicious.

Lieutenant

Nah, he looks harmless enough. Anyway, I need to shove off for a bit, so you just stay put and keep an eye on things here while I'm gone. Go ahead—hop on out of my car.

Tralf

(Exiting the vehicle.) Where are you going?

Lieutenant

I just remembered an important meeting I've got at the Pants on Fire Club, but you stay right here—don't go anywhere. (The Lieutenant's car can be heard driving away as the stage lights fade.)

Scene III

(In the basement of McGuffin's building outside a boiler room. A man can be seen in the dark room on the opposite side of the stage assembling some equipment near a large furnace.)

Lieutenant

You gettin' anything on the infrareds, Sergeant? How many perps can you make out?

Sergeant

It's the boiler room, sir. I'm only reading oranges and reds.

Lieutenant

We got any schematics on that furnace, Captain? What type is it?

Captain

This is a vintage building. That furnace is so old they didn't have types when it was installed. They're replacing it next month with a geothermal heat pump. (Nervous pause.) The super also said back in the twenties fathers of unwed flappers would creep down here in the middle of the night to throw their daughters' newborn bastards into that thing.

Lieutenant

Thanks for the fun fact, Cap.

Sergeant

So are we going in now or waiting for a SWAT detail?

Captain

Lieutenant, I'll leave the call to you.

Lieutenant

Your guy said he just saw the one towel head with a backpack skulking around down here in the basement?

Sergeant

Yes, sir. But he wasn't wearing a towel on his head.

Lieutenant

Pretty observant—sounds like the guy I tailed over here…he wasn't wearing a towel either. Could he say what made the backpack look suspicious?

Sergeant

No, sir—except that it was on the back of a towel head in a building full of rich people.

Lieutenant

Let's hope there's just one in there, and let's hope we're not about to scare the soul out of some poor plumber. Sergeant, when I kick the door open you hit the high-beam on your flashlight. Maybe we can blind him instead of shoot him. On three. One. Two. Now!

(The door bursts open with a kick from the Lieutenant and the boiler room is filled with light from the Sergeant's high-powered flashlight, revealing the Bomber assembling a bomb near the furnace.)

Lieutenant

Stop right there goddamn it!

(The Bomber holds up a small detonator.)

Captain

I guess he's not the plumber.

Lieutenant

Drop it or I'll shoot you in your face!

Bomber

(In broken English.) To hell with you!

(Tralf emerges from the shadows behind the furnace, calmly walks unnoticed behind the Bomber to the bomb and pulls the firing pin. He then walks into the midst of the standoff.)

Lieutenant

Tralf, you followed me here?

Tralf

I did not; my taxi driver did. I could have gotten you in building faster had I been with you.

Captain

We're kind of in the middle of a situation here.

Tralf

I would say you are more at end of situation.

Bomber

To hell with you! (He depresses the button atop the detonator. Tralf holds up the now vibrating firing pin.)

Bomber

To hell with you! (He quickly pulls another detonator from his backpack and depresses the button. Tralf pulls another vibrating firing pin from his coat pocket.)

Tralf

I got that one too. (To the Lieutenant.) "Too" with double "o" not double "u."

Bomber

(Quietly with resignation.) To hell with you.

Scene IV

(Back in the observation room.)

Lieutenant

(Entering from the interrogation room.) This towel head isn't going to give us anything. He probably only speaks Arabic.

Tralf

I think he was speaking Farsi. Also, he is clearly not wearing towel, and if he were it would be called kufiyah, but he probably does not wear kufiyah; he would likely wear turban.

Lieutenant

Ain't you a smart somebody.

Captain

Do you think it was just a coincidence that this guy was trying to blow up McGuffin's building?

Sergeant

I had just left with him for a meeting in the Loop when I got the heads-up from my team at the building.

Lieutenant

Half the penthouses in that building are owned by people who made their fortunes in alternative fuels and green technologies. That's got to piss somebody off. Maybe this camel jockey represents the interests of the camel jockeys who sell us all those barrels of dinosaur juice.
After all, blowing shit up is their version of lobbying.

Tralf

Captain, in my time we have aphorism: there are no coincidences.

Captain

We say the same thing now.

Tralf

I would like to interview him.

Lieutenant

No way.

Captain

Sure, go ahead.

Tralf

Thank you. (Enters the interrogation room.)

Lieutenant

Captain, this has really gone too far.

Captain

What difference does it make? Homeland Security is going to pick this guy up within the hour, and nobody here has been able to get anything out of him. Besides if it wasn't for Tralf, they might be picking your teeth out of my brain right now. At least he knows what language our bad guy speaks.

Sergeant

And the kind of headdress he wears.

Lieutenant

(Indignantly.) What the hell do I know? I'm just a God-fearing tax-payer.

Tralf

(Entering the interrogation room.) Hello. (Sits down across from the Bomber.)

Bomber

(In broken English.) To hell with you!

Tralf

(Comfortingly.) I am not police officer. I took their test once, but I did not pass. Lieutenant who you were just chatting with thinks you wear kufiyah, but I know you likely wear turban. I know another man who wears turban. I have met many interesting people during my time here; they have sought me out from all corners of globe. I am going to send this man your picture. I also need audio sample from you. (Tralf pulls a phone from his coat and snaps a photo of the Bomber.)

Bomber

To hell with you!

Tralf

That will do. Now we just have to wait few moments. (Tralf sends the information on his phone, and then the two sit in silence for a long moment, the bewildered Bomber staring at his composed interrogator. The phone chimes.) Here we are. (Tralf scrolls through some text.) According to other man who wears turban you studied Civil Engineering for two years at University of Illinois, so it seems likely that you speak more English than "To hell with you," though between you and me I do not much care for their language either, such as it is. It reads here that you dropped out of college after your father was assassinated. I am sorry for your loss.

That is when you joined organization with which you are currently affiliated. Here is image of your mother; she has kind eyes. See? (Tralf shows the Bomber the image on the phone's screen.) Here is image of your sister, though it is bit pixilated. Nevertheless, I am sure she is pretty. (Shows him the screen again.) And here is image of your little brother. He was crippled by landmine while playing soccer—that is shame. (Shows him the screen again.)

This man I know who wears turban knows other people. He knows man who wears pakol that would take your mother and put her to work processing his poppy crops into opium. He is not benevolent boss. He does not provide health care for his employees or give them time off. He works his employees dozen and half hours every day. If his employees stop working, he stops feeding them until they resume work or die. He has high turnover rate.

This man I know who wears turban knows another man who wears fez, though they call it tarboosh where he is from and they have not been in fashion for quite some time, but this man is bit of anachronism. He will take your sister and put her to work in his house of ill repute. If she does not earn money she will be sold to whomever.

This man I know who wears turban knows another man who hires himself out to perform callous tasks. He will drag your paraplegic brother into street and fire two bullets into his head. I see here your little brother was named after your now mar-tyred father. Man who would do this to your brother does not wear hat, but he sometimes wears helmet.

Woman I loved lived in building you attempted to raze. She is dead now. She was murdered. I know you had nothing to do with her death, but thought of her killing fills me with such rage that I do not care who I hurt when I chose to articulate my anger. Perhaps you can empathize. Tell me everything, or I will have this man I know who wears turban proceed. Choice is yours. (Threateningly.) I am not police officer.

Bomber

Okay.

ACT TWO

Scene I

(Tralf is sitting on a park bench. In the dark half of the stage the two FBI agents are meeting with the Blographer.)

Tralf

(In deep concentration, sending his noon report. The Lieutenant enters, approaches Tralf, and stands in front of him as he speaks.)

Colloquialisms favor brevity over accuracy.
Example: mobile phones are

more commonly known as cell phones, despite
that their salient feature is not their

cellular signals but rather their mobility. Also, phones
are more often used for emailing, Interneting,

and texting than calls.

Out.

Lieutenant

(As Tralf finishes, the Lieutenant snaps his fingers and Tralf comes out of his daze, noticing the Lieutenant.) E.T. phone home, huh?

Tralf

(Tralf moves over and the Lieutenant sits.) My apologies, I did not see you standing there. I was transmitting my noon report.

Lieutenant

Funny, I thought your reports would be more…noteworthy, but I guess if you gotta send two a day they're not all gonna be earthshattering. I know how paperwork can be…never ending.

Tralf

Yes.

Lieutenant

That was some pretty deep trance shit though.

Tralf

Yes.

Lieutenant

So this is the place that perp you put the screws to said he meets his contact?

Tralf

Yes.

Lieutenant

I got the invitation to your Doubleday shindig tonight. You invited the Captain and Sergeant too, huh?

Tralf

Yes.

Lieutenant

Would you stop answering all of my questions by just saying yes?

Tralf

Yes.

Lieutenant

You can be a real pain in the ass almost all of the time. So what's this Doubleday event about?

Tralf

I use portion of proceeds from my book to throw monthly social gathering, at which I observe human interactions in more convivial setting. I glean great insight from less-guarded conversations. As for event's name, I receive royalty payments from my publisher every second day of week of every second week of month. I find that more people are free on Tuesday nights.

Lieutenant

It's a real chore to listen to you talk. Wait a minute—I thought today was Monday.

Tralf

No, it is second day of week of second week of month.

Lieutenant

Right, Monday is the second day of the week, since Sunday is the first day.

Tralf

How could Sunday be first day of week and also be part of weekend?

Lieutenant

What the hell do you know? You probably think there ought to be twelve days a week.

Tralf

Yes. I thought of good stakeout question for you, since we both enjoy baseball. If you were concessions vendor at ballpark, would you rather sell peanuts, hot dogs, or beer? If you sold peanuts, you could throw bags, which would be fun. However, if you sold hot dogs, you could make that cacophonic yet strangely pleasant banging noise with lid of warmer container, which is part of ambient symphony in grandstands. But then if you sold beer you would be most popular vendor of all.

Lieutenant

(Not paying any attention to the question.) Shit, today is Tuesday, isn't it? Jesus, I should've known. I hate Tuesdays. I always have. You know what I hate most about Tuesdays? They're inevitable. You never go to bed Monday night and wake up on a Saturday morning...or even a Wednesday morning. People think Monday's the worst day of the week, but it's really Tuesday, because it comes after the worst day of the week but it ain't no better.

Tralf

Did your wife leave you on Tuesday?

Lieutenant

Why the hell did you have to go and bring a thing like that up?

Tralf

Your anger over day of week seems irrational. I thought perhaps you were projecting your anger about some event that occurred on Tuesday to day itself.

Lieutenant

Well maybe so, but it's better than focusing my anger on pedestrians, or the Chicago Flubs, or you for that matter. (Pause.) So yes, she left me on a Tuesday. That's my point. Bad shit always happens to me on Tuesdays. My life's a long turd of Tuesdays shat from the devil's anus. It's been that way ever since I was born and it'll be that way until the day I die. From cradle to grave.

Tralf

That is odd expression—cradle to grave. Why not rhyming womb to tomb or alliterative crib to coffin?

Lieutenant

(Quietly.) I hope her child is born with twenty toes and no fingers.

Tralf

Pardon?

Lieutenant

Nothing…it's just that I found out she's pregnant again by her fiancé—the osteopath.

Tralf

I understand your disappointment, but wishing such fate on her unborn child seems gratuitously spiteful.

Lieutenant

What—she leaves me, and now I have to be a good sport about it? What would a head-case like you know anyhow?

Tralf

My wife in my time left me, in manner of speaking.

Lieutenant

She killed herself?

Tralf

Yes.

Lieutenant

So that's how you could leave your time behind. It didn't matter if you were here or there, you'd be alone either way.

Tralf

I never believed I would feel love for another until Mrs. Mc-Guffin.

Lieutenant

(Pause.) I'm depressed—let's go to a ball game.

Scene II

(Inside the tunnel leading to the locker rooms in the bowels of Wrigley Field. The dark portion of the stage is empty.)

Lieutenant

(Urinating against a wall.) Man, I love pissing outdoors.

Tralf

We are not outdoors. We are in tunnel missing bottom of ninth.

Lieutenant

I can see the sky and smell the grass—same difference.

Tralf

You could achieve similar effect by urinating near open window.

Lieutenant

(Zipping and turning toward Tralf. He flashes his badge to unseen onlookers.) Police business— move along.

Tralf

We just missed end of game.

Lieutenant

We missed the last pitch, but not the end of the game. (The Lieutenant leans over the railing near the dark half of the stage just as the other cast members, dressed as baseball players, slowly file through. The Lieutenant begins heckling the silent players.) You gravies hear all that booing? They're not tryin' to scare ya. Hey rookie, you run like a little girl and bat like an old lady. Hey big time, were you gold-brickin' today because you thought the game wasn't being televised? Hey slow, my grandmother throws harder than you. Were you tryin' to wear 'em out for tomor-row's game by letting them hit all those dingers today? Well get in there boys; those fat paychecks ain't gonna cash themselves. Just because you're no good at your job ain't no reason not to be overpaid to do it. (To Tralf as the two exit.) It always makes me feel a little better to hassle somebody that's got a lot more.

Scene III

(At Tralf's Doubleday party. Tralf stands silently with the Captain on one half of the stage as the Blographer and the Sergeant talk in another room on the other half.)

Blographer

(In the middle of a conversation.) So how did you remedy your interior design conundrum?

Sergeant

Bought a futon—now when the bed converts to a couch my studio converts from a bedroom to a living room.

Blographer

I had a futon once. It was the most uncomfortable couch I'd ever sat on and the most uncomfortable bed I'd ever slept in. (Laughing unctuously.)

Lieutenant

(Entering.) I can't tell if you're the worst fake laugher I've ever heard or just an idiot...wait now I can. Nothin' taste better than free booze. (Holding up a fifth of whiskey.) Say there Henry Wadsworth Shortfellow, El Capitan wants a word with you, unless you'd rather go play with yourself on the Sarge's crouton.

Blographer

Sheathe thy rapier like wit, for truly there is no defense against it.

Lieutenant

My old man once told me that ninety percent of everything in this life is crap, and I think you're just the guy who's gonna make sure we meet that quota.

Sergeant

He's coarse but clever.

Blographer

If you say so. I want to make it clear once more before I take my leave that Mister Tralf welcomes you to this Doubleday occasion and sincerely hopes that you enjoy yourselves, but remember he is here as an observer and is not to be spoken to. In fact, his only wish at these soirees is for his guests to ignore him completely.

Lieutenant

Ignoring that dude is like trying to ignore a fungus growing on your face. (Raising his voice.) He might as well wear an elephant costume.

Blographer

You should maybe lower your voice.

Lieutenant

(Making his voice deeper.) He might as well wear an elephant costume.

Blographer

Very droll.

Lieutenant

Is that your way of saying "funny," William Butler Yikes?

Blographer

Did you go to a library for like the first time ever today?

Lieutenant

Hey, I went to college too you know. I rarely went to class, but I went to college.

Blographer

Yes, well we'll have to continue this battle of wits later. I shall now inquire what your good Captain needs of me...perhaps some help with a case. (Exiting to the other room with Tralf and the Captain.)

Lieutenant

I'll plead the fifth on that. (Holding up the bottle.) Don't hurry back. (To the Sergeant.) Man, the world is full of somebodies, but he sure ain't one of 'em.

Sergeant

So what does Cappy want him for?

Lieutenant

How the hell should I know? I haven't talked to him all night. He's probably closer to the bottom of his bottle than I am, but then he's got more years on the job than me. (Sounding intoxicated.) I think this sensitive disco-folk music is either gonna make me go gay or deaf.

Sergeant

I like the music.

Lieutenant

Yeah, me too. You know, you're not like other women—always running their mouths about stupid stuff.

Sergeant

What kind of stuff?

Lieutenant

I dunno…gossip at work or some dumb-ass dream they had the night before. (Mocking) Oh really, then what did your dead grandfather say to the rabbit in the top hat?

Sergeant

We know all the same work gossip, and I talk about my dreams with somebody else. You have a lady-friend, don't you? Do you think you'll ever get married again?

Lieutenant

Maybe…when I start to lose my looks, so probably in my late nineties.

(The Blographer talking with the Captain in the other room. The stage lighting should toggle back and forth between the two conversations.)

Blographer

(Finishing a diatribe about who knows what.) For it's the provincial who long for the past, and the naïve who yearn for the future.

Captain

I can tell you're well educated, but I believe that intelligence is what you say, and education is how you say it. Anyone who thinks differently has too little of one and too much of the other.

Blographer

Possibly…I'll have to give that some thought.

Captain

I think I'm beginning to see the appeal of Tralf's story. It's good to hear that a future exists--that the human race has endured; however, it's also comforting to know that they have their own problems. It would be too much to bear the idea of having missed out on paradise by being born a few generations too early.

(Other room.)

Lieutenant

You look like a crook in that dress.

Sergeant

Why's that?

Lieutenant

Because when I first saw you in it, you stole my breath.

Sergeant

Thanks…I guess, but aren't you a little over the hill to be hitting on me?

Lieutenant

Hell, I ain't even begun to approach the summit. Is your dress made out of donkey tobacco?

Sergeant

What?

Lieutenant

Because I want to smoke that ass.

Sergeant

Now you're just being straight-up inappropriate.

Lieutenant

Well let's not dwell on it.

Sergeant

Listen, boss, you should behave yourself and ease up on the free booze.

(Other room.)

Blographer

(Offering an answer to an unheard question.) There are two reasons a writer doesn't like to discuss his work. Firstly, the work isn't a riddle with one right answer; every reader should arrive at their own independent conclusion. Secondly, the work, if written well, should speak for itself.

Captain

I just wanted to know the name of your blog.

Blographer

I apologize Captain…I misunderstood your question. Are you feeling okay? You look a little tired…or intoxicated.

Captain

(Slurring his speech.) If I'm inebriated then I've earned it… comes with doing what I do and seeing what I've seen. I'm a fourth generation cop.

Blographer

That's impressive.

Captain

It's not impressive; it's unoriginal. I'm playing a role. The characters keep changing but not the plot. I lock up bad guys so other bad guys can take their place. I'm not enforcing law and order; I'm creating opportunities.

Blographer

I don't think the victims of the people you've put away would see it like that.

Captain

When I joined the force, there was this serial killer called the Cruel Clown. You remember him?

Blographer

That was before my time, but I've read about him online. He murdered thirty or so teenage boys and buried their bodies under his house.

Captain

Yeah, real genius that one. Did that web site also happen to say who caught him?

Blographer

Not that I recall.

Captain

The Des Plaines police department got credit for the collar. You know anything about Des Plaines?

Blographer

It's the home of the first franchised McDonald's.

Captain

Yeah, and it wasn't the home of the Clown. Do you think it odd that the cops in Des Plaines got the drop on that serial killer when most of the boys were abducted from here in the city, which has a police force of over 12,000 officers?

Blographer

I guess…maybe.

Captain

Take my word for it. This Clown was known to us, but we didn't arrest him because we couldn't make a case. Did you also know that some of the Clown's victims went missing while he was documented to be out of the state?

Blographer

He had accomplices?

Captain

Officially no, because the script demanded that there be only one murdering psychopath. There has to be one every now and then, or else it wouldn't make sense that we have a concept for it, but nobody could stomach the thought of a confederacy of serial killers.

Blographer

But you're saying there were more.

Captain

I'm saying if there were more, then they were definitely known to us too, but we couldn't make a case against them either. So when we caught the one, we were told to stop going after the rest. We struck an unspoken deal with the Clown's accomplices to cease and desist, letting them walk away and forcing us to pretend that the prospect of a not guilty verdict was the same as innocence.

Blographer

And it worked?

Captain

So far as we know, but it ain't exactly the kind of justice that one goes into law enforcement for…rather an expedient compromise. The sort of half measure that gives the air you breathe a putrid taste.

Blographer

That's quite a story Captain. Can I quote you on that?

Captain

You can go pound sand. (Exits.)

(Other room.)

Lieutenant

(Sidling closer to the Sergeant.) We see so much ugliness on the job. We should take this opportunity to make something beautiful together—like two ships that go bump in the night.

Sergeant

Personal space is supposed to be just longer than your reach.

Lieutenant

I'm willing to share my space with you. (The Lieutenant puts his arm around her waist.)

Sergeant

Get your hand off me right now.

Lieutenant

I'm sorry, I thought that was my hip.

Sergeant

I have a boyfriend, you know.

Lieutenant

There's nothin' more boring in this whole world than a pretty girl with a boyfriend. (The Lieutenant leans in for a kiss and the Sergeant throws her drink in his face and exits.)

Scene IV

(At a stakeout again, Tralf sits contemplatively alone on the park bench. After a few moments the Lieutenant approaches with a sack of food and sits down. McGuffin sits smoking in the dark half of the stage.)

Lieutenant

You stare any harder you're gonna go blind.

Tralf

I was thinking of something.

Lieutenant

Well, blink once in a while. You're creepin' me out. Here I got you some victuals from the Middle Eastern place down the block. (The two begin eating.)

Tralf

(Examining the spork in his hand.) What is this utensil called?

Lieutenant

That's your silverware. It's a spork. You know a spoon and fork put together.

Tralf

(Using the spork to eat.) It does not effectively impale solids… or adequately contain liquids. It is made of plastic, why do you call it silverware?

Lieutenant

I don't know. They used to be made of silver and the name just stuck. Call it flatware if it suits you better.

Tralf

But it is not flat.

Lieutenant

Jesus, I'm trying to eat here. Put some food in your hole and shut the hell up. What do I look like anyway, the housewares clerk at Sears? (Eating.) This falafel tastes like ass, which is ironic I guess since it ain't got no meat in it.

(After a moment of quiet eating.)

Lieutenant

Look at that over there…the bum pissing on that Mercedes— funny.

Tralf

This city is home to such wealth and such poverty.

Lieutenant

People make their choices.

Tralf

Yes, but do people not deserve second chances?

Lieutenant

Sure, everybody deserves a second chance, so long as it don't interfere with somebody else's first chance.

Tralf

This time's inequity of wealth does not trouble you?

Lieutenant

If everybody was paid a living wage, a Big Mac would cost fifteen bucks.

Tralf

If wealth were distributed equitably, fifteen dollars would be fair price.

Lieutenant

I don't make the rules.

Tralf

Nor do I, but it seems we both follow them.

Lieutenant

Cages without bars. A wise man once said, "He who knows how will always work for he who knows why."

Tralf

Jean-Paul Sartre?

Lieutenant

David Lee Roth. (Pause.) So I gotta smooth things over with the Sarge after my behavior last night.

Tralf

Give her flowers.

Lieutenant

No, that doesn't seem right. She's more into guns than roses.

Tralf

Then give her gun.

Lieutenant

Giving an angry woman a gun is never a good idea. Besides, I can't afford to buy her anything until payday. I went to the OTB after your party last night and lost a bunch of dough. That hooch you served has gotta be the most expensive free booze I ever drank.

Tralf

Do you gamble often?

Lieutenant

Not anymore. I gambled most of my money away after the divorce. I was drinking pretty heavy back then, and one vice fed the other. You know how it is, you go on a bender until you finally wake up in a pool of your own vomit, only to find out you bet the rent on the home team the night before. Last night was just a slip.

Tralf

I am confused by your behavior at Wrigley Field yesterday, which do you consider to be the home team—White Sox or Cubs?

Lieutenant

I back 'em both unless they play each other. Then I hope all the cars of the Sox players get repossessed and their only means of transportation to the ballpark are stilts and unicycles—a parade in pinstripe marching along the LSD.

Tralf

Yes, that would be sight. (Pause.) I do know how it is, as you say. I struggle with my appetites in this time.

Lieutenant

You ain't got addiction in your time?

Tralf

Any genetic predisposition for addiction is purged of course. However, in this body I feel...urges.

Lieutenant

Why Tralf...you freak. You're not a bad looking guy. If you kept all that time-traveling mumbo- jumbo to yourself, you could probably score with all kinds of ladies—or at least the kind that ain't too particular.

Tralf

It seems wrong to make love with woman that I do not love.

Lieutenant

Maybe I ain't got as much compunction on that point as I should. It'd be easier for me to be more humane in that regard if it weren't for my human nature. Did you and Mrs. McGuffin ever get it on?

Tralf

She loved me, but would not make love with me because of vow she made to her philandering husband.

Young FBI Agent

(Approaching with a twitch.) Smoke?

Lieutenant

What?

Young FBI Agent

You holding?

Lieutenant

Beat it punk.

Young FBI Agent

You beat it. You're sittin' on my mother-fucking bench, mother fucker.

Lieutenant

Listen shit head, I'm a cop.

Young FBI Agent

So what, I'm FBI?

Lieutenant

I ought to warn you that I'm hungover, so if you make me gun up, I'm only gonna aim for your thigh, but with the shakes I got I might accidently drill you in the kneecap instead, or maybe I'll miss the other way and shoot off your pecker.

Old FBI Agent

(Approaching from behind, catching Tralf and the Lieutenant unawares.) You talk too much. I don't think I like you.

Lieutenant

Lots of people don't like me. What makes you special?

Old FBI Agent

(Pushing an object in his coat pocket into the Lieutenant's back.) I don't like you, and I have a gun pointed at your spine.

Young FBI Agent

(No longer twitching.) What's his deal? (Gesturing to Tralf with an object in the pocket of his sweatshirt.)

Lieutenant

Who him? People don't like him either.

Young FBI Agent

Let's shoot off their thumbs.

Old FBI Agent

Nah, let's shoot out their eyes.

Lieutenant

I'd rather you shot off our ears, so we don't have to listen to anymore of your pretend tough guy talk. (To Old FBI Agent.) You mind moving the barrel of that gun from my neck?

Old FBI Agent

A loaded gun aimed at your back makes you nervous, huh?

Lieutenant

Hell, that ain't no big thing. I just don't want my chiropractor upset with me.

Old FBI Agent

(Pulling a bottle of water from his coat pocket.) Relax cowboy, it's only a bottle of water.

Young FBI Agent

(Revealing the object in his sweatshirt pocket to be a sandwich.) You caught us at lunch, too.

Lieutenant

So you dip shits really are Feds—that's just dandy. Well anyway, we're in the midst of an investigation, so off you go.

Old FBI Agent

You're conducting an investigation into the disappearance of a local; we're conducting an investigation with international implications.

Young FBI Agent

And your pissant investigation is interfering with our global investigation.

Lieutenant

Global investigation with international implications…my, that all sounds so impressive. You fellas must have dual citizenship in Loserville and Lametown.

Old FBI Agent

Good one, Walt Witty-man.

Lieutenant

What's that you say? I think you've been talking to a guy we know.

Old FBI Agent

Look here, I hate to pull rank—

Lieutenant

You probably enjoy pulling rank as much as you like pulling on your boyfriend's peter. We'll just see what my captain has to say about all this juris-prick-tion nonsense.

Young FBI Agent

Your boss isn't our boss.

Lieutenant

Lord, I wish I'd shot you when I had the chance.

Scene V

(The FBI Agents, Tralf, and the Lieutenant are standing silently in the interrogation room. The Captain is on the phone in the room opposite with the Sergeant standing nearby.)

Sergeant

(Entering the interrogation room.) Can somebody tell my why the hell I just got pulled off my detail? The captain is on the phone with the superintendent, and I heard that there are some Feds snooping around. (Noticing the FBI Agents.) Oh.

Tralf

Allow me to introduce Special Agent Wynken and Special Agent Blynken.

Lieutenant

They work very closely together…usually in the dark. (Quietly to the Sergeant.) Hey, I wanted to tell you that I'm sorry for—

Sergeant

(Quietly.) Hey, hey yourself…I know you're sorry, and you're also forgiven, but don't let it happen again, or next time I'll fire a warning shot…through your thick skull.

Young FBI Agent

(To Tralf after an awkward silence.) You knew the bomber spoke Farsi, right? You cracked him good. By the time we got him he was singing like a chair.

Sergeant

Like a chair?

Tralf

He meant to say "choir." He confused vowel. It is common mistake for non-native speakers.

Young FBI Agent

You wrote, *Dozavo*, didn't you? I read it.

Lieutenant

So, you're into poetry?

Young FBI Agent

Not exactly, his file came across my desk recently.

Lieutenant

You've got a file on this guy?

Old FBI Agent

We've got a file on everybody.

Lieutenant

You got a file on me?

Old FBI Agent

We've got a file on everybody that's anybody...sorry, you didn't make the cut.

Captain

(Entering.) I just got off the phone with the superintendent. I'm afraid we'll have to desist with our investigation for the time being.

Lieutenant

Bull, horse, and chicken shit!

Old FBI Agent

It's imperative to our investigation, and national security as it happens, that McGuffin takes his trip to Japan believing himself to be above suspicion. Be assured though that we will have him under constant surveillance.

Young FBI Agent

We have reason to believe that he is in league with some nefarious factions, and he may be disinclined to keep his meetings with said factions if you spook him.

Old FBI Agent

We'll share any information we can that might assist with your investigation upon our return.

Lieutenant

If this is such a circle jerk, how come we're the only ones with sticky hands?

Old FBI Agent

(To the Captain.) You've got a real crackerjack team here. We'll be in touch. (The FBI Agents exit.)

Sergeant

This isn't right. Somebody has to do something.

Lieutenant

We're somebodies, ain't we?

Captain

What did you have in mind?

Lieutenant

Me and lucky go over to McGuffin's place with our hats in our hands and our heads hung low and tell him that he got the better of us. Maybe he gloats and lets something spill. Hell, maybe we get him to sing like an electric chair, and maybe we just record the whole conversation.

Sergeant

That's the oldest trick in the book.

Lieutenant

That's why it's worth a try; it's so old it's new again.

Tralf

Am I lucky in your scenario?

Lieutenant

That remains to be seen.

Captain

You're mistaken, Sergeant. The oldest trick in the book would be simply to beat a confession out of him. I'd say good luck to you two, but I officially know nothing of your plan.

Scene VI

(Tralf and the Lieutenant enter a hallway in McGuffin's penthouse and encounter the Blographer exiting McGuffin's study. McGuffin is sitting and smoking in his lit study, revealing him as the man who was in the dark room during scene 4.)

Lieutenant

Hey look, it's old what's-his-nuts. You've been selling your ass to the Feds and McGuffin —an industrious little whore, ain't you?

Blographer

(Ignoring the Lieutenant.) Mister Tralf, I did not realize you were here.

Tralf

For some reason, I thought you might be.

Lieutenant

You put that together too, huh?

Blographer

I chronicled your story for the world, but recently your following has dwindled, despite my efforts to make you a more compelling character. I don't think the world believes your narrative anymore…I'm not sure I do either.

Lieutenant

Hear that? He thinks you're just a flash in the pan.

Tralf

(To the Lieutenant.) Spark in skillet works better. (To the Blographer.) So now you will make up lies about McGuffin? You can evade truth temporarily, but never permanently.

Blographer

Just as you endeavor to improve your future, I must do likewise for my own. Mister McGuffin has agreed to give me exclusive access to his exploits. I may one day be the President's personal biographer. I'm…sorry.

Lieutenant

Take a walk parasite. (The Blographer exits.) Okay, just follow my lead. I'll get him talking about how we ain't come up with nothing, but that we've got one last lead to explore. Maybe we'll get him to ask some questions that we can turn back on him. How do you feel—loose?

Tralf

I feel as if we are on precipice of denouement.

Lieutenant

Good. Sure. Whatever. (Knocking on the door to McGuffin's study.)

McGuffin

Enter. (Closely watching the Lieutenant and Tralf as they enter through the study's scorched oak door.) Ah, the intrepid investigators are here to pay me a visit. How goes the search for my missing wife?

Lieutenant

Not well at all. We've turned up less than nothing. The sergeant tells me that the kidnappers haven't contacted you either.

McGuffin

No ransom demands have been made as of yet—most peculiar.

Lieutenant

Yes—most peculiar indeed. (Eyeing the study door.)

McGuffin

I see the door to my study has caught your eye, Lieutenant. That was the very door to Sir Walter Raleigh's cell just before he was beheaded at Whitehall. It was one of the few items to survive the fire there, though not unscathed as you can see.

Lieutenant

Seems like a rich guy like you could afford a new door.

McGuffin

I have heard reports of your wit; however, I fear it has not benefited your investigation.

Tralf

(Becoming enraged.) You have played us well, but game is at end. Take satisfaction in knowing that you beat us, though it will be a Pyrrhic victory. Now confess and accept punishment.

Lieutenant

(Quietly to Tralf.) Easy fella, you're going off script.

McGuffin

Why Tralf, you surprise me—

Tralf

People of my time will think like you, believing themselves to be above laws of man and nature. People like you murder my future. They will be made to pay for their hubris, and so shall you.

McGuffin

I doubt it…but now I need to prepare for my trip, so I'll have to ask you both to leave.

Lieutenant

We'll leave, but don't think this is over. Come on, Tralf. (The Lieutenant grabs the unmoving Tralf by the arm and attempts to lead him through the study door.) I guess for your sake it's good that you're comfortable behind prison doors.

McGuffin

Tralf, take solace in the fact that my wife achieved her lifelong wish to leave the world better than she found it. After all, her departure from it has slightly reduced our global carbon footprint.

Tralf

(Tralf pushes the Lieutenant out of the study, slams the door shut, turns the skeleton key in the lock, and puts the key in his pocket. He crosses the room to a wall display of crossed rapiers and grabs one with each hand.) Right or left?

McGuffin

Come now, you can't be serious. You expect me to duel with you?

Tralf

If you do not defend yourself, then stabbing you to death will be much simpler for me. Which one?

Lieutenant

(Banging on the door.) Tralf, damn you, open this door right now.

Tralf

This is first time in my life I've ever held weapon of any kind. I have no training in violence. I know you fenced in college and you will almost certainly win this contest, but I can no longer abide your existence on this earth. One of us must be dispatched from it. Choose.

McGuffin

The left one then. (Tralf places the rapier in his left hand on the desk before McGuffin. McGuffin rises, and the two set to dueling.)

Lieutenant

(Still banging on the door.) Tralf, stop right now. We can still burn this guy in court.

McGuffin

(The two trade several cuts.) You have quickness but no technique.

Lieutenant

(Hammering the butt of his gun against the door's iron hinges.) Tralf, just let me in and I'll put a bullet in his head. We'll say he flipped out and came at you with the sword.

McGuffin

(Near the door.) That's not very sporting of you Lieutenant. (To Tralf.) You should know that the last word my wife said was your name. (Tralf charges McGuffin in a rage. McGuffin runs Tralf through with his rapier. Tralf slumps to the floor against the door.) Your man is down. You had better call for an ambulance.

Tralf

Last man standing is not always victor. (Tralf grabs McGuffin's ankle as he walks near the door and slices his ACL, causing him to topple to the floor. Tralf crawls toward McGuffin and slits his throat.) It is finished.

Lieutenant

(Hanging up his mobile phone.) Tralf, the ambulance is on the way. Is he dead?

Tralf

Yes.

Lieutenant

Okay, we'll just say it was self-defense. That was a pretty good idea to play possum like that.

Tralf

(Holding his bloodied chest.) Yes, good idea.

Lieutenant

(Examining the floor.) Tralf, there's a lot of blood coming under the door. Are you sure you're all right.

Tralf

I am fine, but I am dying.

Lieutenant

Tralf, open the door.

Tralf

(Tralf pulls the key from his pocket but cannot reach the lock.)
I cannot.

Lieutenant

That's okay—just slide the key under the door.

Tralf

Prison doors only have locks on one side. I suppose that makes
you prisoner.

Lieutenant

(Sliding to the floor against the door.) Stay with me. The ambulance should be here any minute.

Tralf

I think this is my last minute.

Lieutenant

Tralf, talk to me. Just keep talking. Hey, how many hairs did
that redhead have anyway?

Tralf

(Losing consciousness.) Same number as visible stars seen from
dark side of moon.

Lieutenant

Tralf, can you still hear me?

Tralf

When I was someone else in this body I would see myself in my sleep…waiting to be reborn. I am only living person who chose to be born. I am only living person who will die twice. Death is not so bad. Never despair of possibility of another life.

Lieutenant

Tralf, damn you, hang on in there!

Scene VII

(The Lieutenant stands alone in the lit section of the stage. The other actors stand listening in the dark half of the stage. The Lieutenant looks at his watch and then to see if anyone is watching him.)

Lieutenant

This is stupid. No one is even listening.

I guess that's a good thing though or people would think I am just as crazy as he was.

I wanted you to know that he did not fail. He did not self-murder.

He loved that woman and avenged her death with his own. He was a

man of our time.

And he was my friend.

Out.

About the Author

Wes Payton has a B.A. in Rhetoric/Philosophy and an M.A. in English. He has been a short-story presenter for the Illinois Philological Association. His play *Way Station* was selected for a Next Draft reading in 2015, and *What Does a Question Weigh?* was selected for a staged reading as part of the 2017 Chicago New Work Festival. He is the author of the novels *Lead Tears*, *Darkling Spinster*, *Darkling Spinster No More*, and *Standing in Doorways*. Wes and his family live in Oak Park, Illinois.

www.ingramcontent.com/pod-product-compliance
Lightning Source LLC
Chambersburg PA
CBHW032225080426
42735CB00008B/724